The 44
Most Com[mon]
Manageme[nt]
Mistakes
And How to
Avoid Them

The 44 Most Common Management Mistakes

And How to Avoid Them

John Courtis

BRITISH INSTITUTE
OF MANAGEMENT

Kogan Page

Published in association with British Institute
of Management and the Institute of Chartered
Accountants in England and Wales

© 1986 John Courtis

Illustrations © Joe Stockton

First published in 1986 by the Institute of Chartered Accountants in England and Wales

First published in 1988 by
Kogan Page Ltd,
120 Pentonville Road, London N1 9JN
in association with British Institute of Management,
Management House, Cottingham Road, Corby, Northants NN17 1TT
and the Institute of Chartered Accountants in England and Wales,
Chartered Accountants' Hall, Moorgate Place, London EC2P 2BJ

Printed and bound in Great Britain by
Biddles Ltd, Guildford

British Library Cataloguing in Publication Data
Courtis, John
   The 44 most common management
   mistakes and how to avoid them.
   1. Management
   I. Title   II. British Institute of
   Management
   658

   ISBN 1-85091-623-3

Acknowledgements

Several chapters draw on material originally published in UK accounting and management journals. We are indebted to Chapter Three Publications, Morgan Grampian and World Media for permission to reproduce them.

Contents

	Page
Introduction	ix
1 The right attitude	1
Blameless behaviour	1
The bright side	4
Offensive action	8
Letting go	8
Making exceptions	9
The long and the short of it	10
Luck	12
The clear desk	13
2 The right people	15
Selecting staff: seventy deadly sins	15
Hiring for profit	20
Keeping people	21
Candidates are customers	23
Signing on	23
Success through succession	27
Directorship delusion	29
The most important budget	31
Secretaries	33
3 Making money	35
Profitable employment	35
Revealing all	36
The penetration obsession	38
Price resistance	40
Paying compensation	42
Growing pains	43

Keeping the company doctor away   44
Management in adversity   47
Panic   50
Overdoing it   50
Needs mustn't   52
Best practice   52
Carry on regardless   53
Negative planning   53
Inaction   55
A retired policeman and a dog   55
The perfect crime   58

4 Communication rules – OK?   60
Gossip abhors a vacuum   61
Effective writing   63
Brevity is the whole of it   67
Four letter words   68
Annual reports   69
MIS   71
Junk mail   73
Bad form   76
Phone blocks   78
The last word   80

Introduction

Most management theory is to be mistrusted. Not because it is wrong, but because too often it is impractical. There is no point in absorbing and trying to apply the heights of academic excellence at one end of the company, if extremely basic and essential management principles are being flouted everywhere else.

This book is about one basic principle which is often neglected. The concept is simple. It is to learn from the mistakes of others. It has several advantages over learning from one's own, but it requires the discipline to identify faults and recognise that one might be duplicating them. Mistakes are opportunities for improvement, and avoiding gratuitous mistakes is more important than gilding the lily on the things you do well. Ideally you can achieve both.

Mistakes can fall crudely into five categories:
1. Errors of omission (failure to act or communicate).
2. Errors of commission (doing things you ought not to have done).
3. Qualitative errors (doing the right thing inadequately or by the wrong method).
4. Errors of timing (doing the right thing too early or too late).
5. Credibility errors (doing the right thing, at the right time, but in such a way as to irritate everyone or discredit the action).

Every one of these can teach us a lesson. All about you, at all levels of contact, people are continually reminding you of the human failings which make good people bad managers. The task is to turn those failings into future virtue. There's a refresher course waiting for you at the office every day.

1
The right attitude

Learning from mistakes can only begin with positive thinking. This section of the book is about the attitudes that turn mistakes into success and create a positive approach which finds ways of making things happen, rather than reasons for doing nothing. It looks at the carrots that are more effective motivators than the sticks—for people, if not for donkeys.

Blameless behaviour

One of the biggest management sticks is the 'culprit' technique. It is practised in most circles, from the academic to the political, and it is infectious. For want of a better scapegoat we could blame schools, where the rot probably starts. But I too have become infected. I wanted to demonstrate that the tendency to rush round looking for a scapegoat is destructive and essentially negative. We should be on our guard, be prepared to identify the malaise and be equipped to cure it. The trouble is that the 'culprit hunt' is a very natural human reaction, but it is only one of several and others are to be preferred. Easy human reactions are often lousy managerially, particularly as managers are always on duty and are not permitted human weaknesses!

Going back to the event which caused the reaction, if something 'goes wrong' there are several possibilities to consider, even before we act practically. The person who looks at only one of these possibilities, without defining the problem or realising the existence of alternatives, is just as dangerous as one who acts without thinking at all. The following possibilities exist for most corporate problems:

1. Nothing is wrong. Somebody has misinterpreted something. (This applies to everything from the fire practice you've forgotten about to the English language whose nuances no two people understand equally.)
2. Human error within your organisation because of incorrect briefing.
3. Human error within, in spite of correct briefing.
4. Error by an outside party.
5. Mechanical failure.
6. Communication failure between outside party (supplier, customer, etc.) and the organisation.
7. Act of God.

The logical application of problem analysis should enable one to react better, because instead of rushing round thinking 'Who the hell . . .', one can rush round thinking 'What the hell . . .' and then, more important, How, Why, Where and When. The Who comes last. The first essential is to determine that a problem exists. The second is to determine the nature of the problem and the remedial action it needs. The third, after any emergency remedies have been decided, must be to determine whether the problem could recur and if preventive action is worthwhile. At this point, and only at this point, does it become necessary to ask 'Who?' in order to plan the constructive side of one's activity properly.

The school system of identifying culprits in order to punish them (to prevent repetition of the offence) very seldom works in business and shouldn't be considered. Unfortunately it works in politics. Culprit identification is a classic political tool. Blaming everything on x years of other party misrule or on anyone and anything other than Government is a standard face-saver, worn somewhat thin by years of use and abuse but nevertheless popular. You can see it applied regularly. The Crown Agents, BSC and the Rent Acts are valid past examples.

We are not politicians. We are managers. We should do better. Once we have identified a problem we can go beyond correction and help to avoid recurrence of this and similar problems by constructive input to the systems and people involved.

No system and no human is foolproof, but every problem gives us the chance to eliminate some of the chances for error. The ideal of course would be to have perfect staff and perfect systems, but in their absence you at least should endeavour to ensure you avoid the sins of misinterpretation, omission and overreaction which add up to management by blame. Next time you find yourself thinking 'Who the hell did . . .' you have a chance to become a better manager.

The school system of identifying culprits . . . seldom works.

Other by-products of management by blame are particularly worrying because they generate complex, costly and irremediable problems where there were none before.

'He's to blame. Fire him!' is illegal and expensive.

'She's to blame. I won't talk to her again' can create anything from a strike to a liquidation via a tribunal.

'It's to blame. Sue the makers' is equally emotional and the one least likely to secure constructive cooperation.

Management by blame is particularly nasty in the management of people. Looking for bad points becomes infectious. Managers whose logic and business decision-making is otherwise impeccable can descend to childish and petty attitudes in their dealings with people. Admittedly there are no perfect humans, so there are no perfect managers, because most managers require both human and technical skills. In practice, senior managers often require more human skills, but have achieved their postion through their technical brilliance.

An environment where people are appraised on their lack of bad points rather than their total of good ones is a recipe for mediocrity. The logical step is to ask how faults can be:
– trained out
– compensated for
– tolerated
– or neutralised

(or whether the environment and job created or aggravated the fault). It is easier to allow for bad points in an outstanding person than train greatness into someone with no bad ones and few good ones. A positive approach to bad points is an incentive to improvement and forewarned will be forearmed. If you still have problems, don't blame me.

The bright side

More money is made, or saved, by getting things right consistently and thoroughly than by wild flights of innovative fancy. A basic management mistake is to assume that errors have occurred without adequate reason for the assumption.

Managers who assume the worst of those about them are allowing specialised hates to damage their analytical ability. When 'something is wrong' there are a number of options to be considered:
1. What is alleged to be wrong really is wrong.
2. Something else is wrong.
3. Nothing is wrong – except one's communications.

The first two options should be self-explanatory. The third is more complex because it offers two quite different alternatives – that something has happened but is not wrong, and that nothing has happened. For example, when my secretary rushed into my office one morning to announce that we had been burgled in the night, I was concerned but not completely convinced. The absence of certain valuable items, the setting of certain locks, marks on the door frames and a door forced open on our co-tenants' premises, all appeared to create the near certainty of a break-in. Fortunately, on enquiry, there were logical reasons for each of these unconnected events. Various things had happened, but we had blindly lumped them together. Nothing was wrong – except our lack of communications.

The second possibility is that nothing has happened. Garbled messages, messages taken out of sequence, symptoms incorrectly observed, facts mistranslated – all of these can conjure up an event from thin air. Put in the hands of a worrier these are tools for creating confusion, although not all the people who assume the worst are necessarily worriers. Some of them have grown up in managerial environments where things did go wrong most of the time, and if you·then transfer them to a department or company where the same pattern of local disaster and crisis is not present, they can be prophets of doom and create massive problems before they realise or are retrained.

This is the key to a wider problem. It is bad enough that someone assumes the worst in an individual case. It is disastrous if a pattern is established, because:

1. It continually obscures the real causes of problems.
2. It delays or prevents corrective action.
3. It demotivates people.
4. It sets a continuing bad example and encourages repetition, because bad managers delegate the task of assuming the worst!

One Ford manager, who always assumed incompetence in his subordinates, spent many weeks trying to find out why the rate of scrap product from a new machine was excessive. His tendency to assume error on the shopfloor was so thoroughly imbued into his team that it was a long time before anyone thought to check whether the machine was capable of working to the tolerances demanded by the new product specification. It wasn't.

This sort of thing is not confined to the shopfloor. Some people do it selectively about suppliers of goods and services, others confine it to their inferiors (a symptom of other management problems), yet others specialise in assuming their bosses are in error. Bad enough when applied outside the organisation, this problem is pernicious and corrosive within because it permanently erodes the victim's position in the eyes of all observers – to everyone's disadvantage. I once worked for a service based company with a ridiculously high staff turnover. One of the reasons it was high was the tendency for the best staff to leave and set up their own competing businesses. The chairman got quite neurotic about this and gradually drifted to a state in which he assumed that almost any sign of disaffection indicated an imminent resignation to start such a business. His 'solution' was to fire the people he suspected.

It will come as no surprise to you, although it came as a continuing surprise to him, that those who were fired turned in desperation to the creation of a competitive business, even if they had not thought of it before, and that those within the company who felt threatened took the precaution of doing the spadework necessary to start one as an insurance against their own enforced departure. This one man created more entrepreneurs in three years than many business schools, but not for the benefit of his shareholders.

Selective pessimists are the most difficult to cope with because they reserve their bias for specific cases. Some are obvious, but the trickiest hide behind a famous saying, 'The customer is always right'. This is the overt or subconscious justification for believing that 'Our company is always wrong'. Sometimes they are right. Sometimes their willingness to accept the possibility of corporate error improves goodwill. Sometimes they will be favourably rated because they appear to be improving customer relations. In spite of this, every pessimist with this particular specialist weakness is a time bomb waiting to explode.

Every time a customer gets a gracious indication of error from the company a precedent is created. The company's image can be damaged as easily as it can be enhanced. Its legal position can be eroded. It can lose money immediately and in the future as a direct consequence. In an extreme case, corporate survival could be threatened. All this because someone has a blind spot about the people around him.

This is not to say that the customer 'is always wrong', or that you should necessarily stick ruthlessly to the letter of your contract in customer negotiation. What is needed is an impartial analysis of the problem and clear discussion with the customer. A customer who may have done something silly with the product should be even more appreciative if given the benefit of the doubt (graciously) than if left to fume in ignorance of the facts. Gracious gestures inadequately understood look like weakness. Better analysis and communication may also mean you don't have to make expensive settlements.

Instead of assuming the worst, the key question is: 'Are we reacting to symptoms or to the real root of the problem?' An emotional response to symptoms cannot match a constructive approach to causes.

Despite the feeling of despair when a car breaks down, statistics show that most breakdowns are due to remarkably simple – and curable – causes. A quick checklist can get you back on the road. The natural state of a motor vehicle is 'in running order'. Give it a little help and it will revert to that state. The same applies to people at work.

Most breakdowns are due to remarkably simple causes . . .

The final message is simple. Most of the time when the company pessimists 'cry wolf', nothing is wrong. Most of the rest of the time it is not as bad as they thought, or it is not what they thought. Better diagnosis and less panic will save you time, money, people, effort and ulcers. Best of all, it costs you nothing to achieve good practice.

Offensive action

Being offensive comes easily to most people, so does being offended. There is a case for not being offended as an essential attitude in good management. The professional manager is being unprofessional in putting the worst construction on an event or not considering the possibility of neutral or benevolent motives behind the action involved. Very often the problem lies in somebody's willingness to be offended rather than in underlying illwill.

Offence is seldom given, it is taken. Don't descend to these levels and you will improve the quality of life around you. You may even find what the 'offender' really meant and benefit from it.

Letting go

There is a popular misconception about delegation. It is that the world is divided into two types; those who delegate and those who do not. This quite dangerous oversimplification obscures the horrid truth that there are three categories:
1. Those who delegate properly.
2. Those who do not delegate at all, either because they are temperamentally incapable of doing so or because they do not understand the concept.
3. The majority, who think they delegate well and fail to do so, with varying degrees of stress for those around them.

The third category includes a wide range of shades of grey, but they all stem from a common fault: a willingness to delegate tasks without delegating the objectives or contexts which make it possible for the subordinate to exercise initiative intelligently.

So, one of two things happen, whether or not the task is

'satisfactorily' completed. Either the subordinate is demotivated (gradually or instantly) or the task is done in the wrong context so that the result is wrong in relation to the organisation's wider interests. For example, a new manager might ask a secretary to arrange for a copy document to be signed by several colleagues and sent urgently by Datapost to a customer some hundreds of miles away. If the secretary knows that a facsimile is acceptable rather than the actual signed bit of paper, the secretary would be able to point out that a Fax transmission facility existed at both ends and save a lot of time and effort. Enormous efforts are wasted in preparing, revising and revising again tasks set by managers. All of which could have been achieved more productively by staff well-informed of their purpose.

Making exceptions

There is a concept in accountancy called exception reporting. It describes the practice of reporting only those aspects of a period's performance which differ significantly from the budgeted levels or ratios. It has very great merit in this primary application, but it also offers a fine example to wider management. The Marks and Spencer group once saved a vast amount of money by treating their goods received/accounts payable functions in this way.

Management by exception assumes that most tasks get done right and on time. Managers should only have to worry about those which will not or do not. This is an extremely simple and effective principle. What is not simple is conditioning people to apply it. Most employees have not been reared this way and certainly have not benefited from it as a management practice under their previous bosses. The conditioning or reconditioning process when you try to introduce it will be long and hard. The system has to be proved by example. It has to be seen to apply to specific tasks and objectives. Then it may have to be rebuilt because somebody above you in the organisation does not understand and has run counter to the flow. Training your boss is part of the process. Setting a good example is too.

In particular, you will have to bridge the gap which people feel because you – or someone else – no longer make hourly contact (albeit for the wrong reasons) and it must be filled correctly. One is tempted to reach for *The One Minute Manager*, but fortunately there is an earlier authority. The late great X. Marcel Boulestin, when describing the relationship which should exist between cooks and mistresses, stressed that the mistress must remember to praise exceptional culinary results. She must also:

> 'mention lightly but firmly what went wrong with that other one. And that for several reasons: the dish must be made correctly next time it is served; the cook must not get away with the illusion that her mistake was not noticed and . . . by saying nothing the mistress would go down in the cook's estimation, which would lead sooner or later to dull, careless or even bad meals. Pleased by compliments, appreciative of just criticism, interested in her work, eager to try new things our cook sees eye to eye with her mistress, who is not of course the kind of woman who when she has said twice a year "that was a very good what's-its-name you gave us the other day" thinks she had done her duty.'

I make no apology for quoting at length from a cookery book by a long dead chef because Boulestin demonstrates very clearly in those few paragraphs that he was also a manager. It is instructive to read what he regards as the preferred results of this process of communication and exception reporting:

> 'The mistress must realise that the interest taken in the dining room is bound to have a good influence on the kitchen. The cook, stimulated and encouraged, will achieve better results. She will feel once more that she is not just a hired servant – that she is in fact part of the household, a human being, with her qualities and failings, but at least a real person, recognized, sharing the interests of her family and treated as part of it.'

If we could all achieve that, for all our employees, with or without exception management, we would have good reasons to be pleased.

The long and the short of it

One of the main differences between managers and other employees is that managers are paid to look beyond the ends of their noses and take a broader view of the company's affairs than the employee meeting narrow targets hourly, daily or weekly.

Ideally it should be possible to test for bad managers by reviewing their sense of proportion and the way they establish priorities but short of persuading them to undertake an 'In-basket' exercise there is no informal way of doing this with any degree of objectivity.

Instead, it may be helpful to list some of the ways managers manage their time and priorities badly, particularly as some of them result from managerial misunderstanding about what is good and bad.

The first problem is the manager who thinks it is possible or desirable to ignore the daily round entirely. Managers actually have to manage daily, earn profits daily, solve problems daily, even if most of the trivia are delegated. By all means encourage delegation and exception reporting but anyone who is totally divorced from the daily affairs of the organisation may just be redundant.

However, at the other end of the scale, the second problem is the manager who recognises to the full the existence of daily demands and is therefore seduced into urgent involvement with trivia which could be delayed, delegated or even ignored. The good manager probably lies somewhere between the two extremes.

The third problem is more subtle. It consists of the important tasks with widely different lead times. Critical path analysis (CPA) has its place in the office as well as in production areas. Only a very good manager never yields to the temptation to tackle a task which will only take a few hours and must be done by tomorrow evening, in preference to starting something which will take many hours in the next four weeks to complete but *must* be started now if it is to be finished on time. The longer the lead time, the greater the temptation to defer a start and the more important it is not to do so.

If you avoid all these errors there is a final test – do you communicate downward and upward enough information about the long lead time plans and priorities to enable subordinates (and superiors) to make their narrower (or wider) decisions in the right context? The shortsighted and the narrowminded walk though their work laying a minefield for their staff, colleagues and successors. These people are not easy to cure from inside the organisation. It can be better to send them on an external time management course and let them discover the principles in private so that they can bring them back almost as their own invention.

In most businesses losing an hour at certain times can lose a day. Some days, if lost, lose a week. Some weeks can lose you a calendar month. Any of them can lose you a decision, a sale, a major contract, an employee or a company.

Luck

Commanders in Chief thoughout history have been quoted as preferring lucky generals to unlucky ones. There is a similar tendency in industry. Employers, press and shareholders develop warm feelings towards senior managers and directors who consistently come up smelling of roses, providing the company concerned is not slipping inexorably into oblivion at the same time. Those managers whose profit centres perform well against all the odds may well be described as lucky.

Luck is bunk. However, what is popularly dismissed as luck, when it is not just coincidence, often hides a degree of forward planning or problem analysis which the owner may be unwilling to share or be doing without fully appreciating the skill involved.

The art, for the management observer, lies in looking behind the luck smokescreen and identifying what other factors are really at work. In my own field I had one colleague who had a remarkable ability to rescue recruitment assignments at the last moment, when the client was being unusually difficult and finding fault with everyone on the primary shortlist. The 'lucky' colleague would almost invariably pull an acceptable extra candidate from about his person and save the day. Not believing in luck, we analysed this and found that long years of dealing with awkward clients had taught the partner in question to interview slightly more people than experience suggested as the right number for client satisfaction, and to keep on interviewing stragglers after the shortlist went in. Hey presto – a supply of suitable late candidates who, as often as not, were forgiven their late application and sometimes even got the job.

In a production environment, people who keep the production lines going when there are materials shortages are not lucky – they have a secret store of work in progress. Someone should look at the cost of that 'comfort stock' before applauding the lucky manager.

The clear desk

One short addendum to arguments about the right attitude: the state of a manager's desk and its reflection on their approach arouses surprising passions in the most unimpassioned people. At one extreme is the hopelessly buried desk, with files spilling onto the floor in a manner reminiscent of a litigation solicitor in the busy season. The author is in this category and defends it as a visual index system.

... the clear desk.

At the other lies the sort of person who, but for a little brass plaque which proclaims that a clear desk is a sign of good management, would have a totally clear desk.

13

Both extremes are wrong of course. The total clutter exponents have failed to read any books on Time Management. The amount of time you can waste looking through piles of paper daily, when the better course is to act on them – or dispose of them, is massive and counter-productive. A little self-discipline would show that constant review is not really improving the quality or quantity of processing. Perhaps some of it could even be delegated.

It is more difficult to criticise the clear desk exponent, but it is necessary. Those of us who are in the messy desk category and know in our hearts that the clear desk is wrong but don't know why, have at last received authoritative support from Bill Reddin, who in the IPM book *The Best of Bill Reddin* states categorically:

'The single best piece of advice I can give to a Chief Executive Officer is to get rid of the desk'.

So there.

2
The right people

Businesses run on money and people. The human resources are usually just as important as the financial ones, and managers need to have people management skills as well as financial ones.

This requirement cannot be delegated to personnel staff. Nobody blames the finance staff for operational failures, just because they are later expressed in financial terms. Similarly, nobody should duck responsibility for people failures just because the personnel staff are the ones who have to draw attention to the results.

People management is real and ever present. It is demanding. Being aware of the need is more than half the battle.

Selecting staff: seventy deadly sins

Having the right people means having the right approach to the selection of staff. We spent several months noting managers' mistakes during the selection process. At the end I had a list – by no means exhaustive – of seventy. All easy to commit.

It is significant that although most of the errors were duplicated or triplicated by several companies, one particular organisation managed to achieve over one third of the total categories on a single assignment. This classic effort was from a company which prides itself on its professionalism in the banking and advisory services it provides for its major international clients! It is also significant that we found the worst error rate among professional partnerships (accountants, solicitors, management consultants, etc.). They manage to combine arrogance, apathy, penny-pinching, poor interviewing and administration indiscipline to a unique extent.

Avoiding selection

1. Assuming a vacancy exists without checking future workload, which may be reducing.
2. Opting for a permanent employee when the peak workloads are temporary and predictable.
3. Failing to check fully whether someone internally can be promoted to the vacancy.
4. Failing to realise that someone internally *wants* the job (and may resign if ignored).

Job analysis

1. Failure to get a correct balance between rewards, candidate requirement and job content.
2. Specifying the (unattainable) ideal candidate rather than the minimum requirements.
3. Failing to recognise at this stage that a compromise from the ideal is likely to be necessary.

Ads, as such

1. Writing glowing advertisements which cannot be supported at interview, thus losing some relevant candidates (who do not reply) and losing the rest at the point of discovery.
2. Believing, with head in sand, that the laws of nature do not apply to one's own advertisements and therefore:
   (a) omitting salary indicator;
   (b) vague or omitted location;
   (c) assuming everyone knows what Joe Bloggs (1971) Ltd. does and how nice it is!
   (d) expecting anyone to write for and complete an application form, whether for a superb job or a menial one, without some further disclosure on the part of the employer – like a job description, company literature, chatty booklet about the new town if relocation is involved, or a warm letter. Any or all of these helps to consolidate the response level;
   (e) not recognising that having someone's name and/or telephone number to reply to converts marginal readers into candidates.

3. Changing the ad, against advice, and then blaming the advisor for failure!
4. Dictating media, against advice, and blaming advisors.
5. Demanding completion of application form when a good c.v. is available.

Choosing and using sources

1. Using a box number without at least giving enough information for potential candidates to know they are not writing to their own employers.
2. Using competing sources without advising them that they are competing against:
   (a) other intermediaries, or
   (b) direct advertising.
   The discovery demotivates candidates *and* intermediaries.
3. Ruining the market with a poor advertisement (or speculative effort with ill-briefed agencies) and then expecting a search or selection firm to save the day later.
4. Switching search consultants in a small close-knit specialist field. (Almost invariably bad PR *and* counter-productive.)
5. Advertising an identifiable job to 'test the market', at the wrong salary or with too limited a brief, thus ensuring all the relevant candidates will read and reject the first ad and ignore the second, even though the latter has got everything right.

Processing people

Direct

1. Slow replies to applications lose candidates.
2. Slow initiation of interview programmes loses people.
3. Uncooperative interview timing loses people.
4. Assuming that candidates are not interested if they do not arrive for interview is incompetence on *your* part. For example:
   (a) These days, the Post Office may have lost a letter to or from you.
   (b) They are on holiday.
   (c) They have been sent away by their employers.
   (d) Your administration went wrong and the interview letter did not go – or the wrong (rejection) letter went – or the time/date was wrong.
   (e) A telephone message to you did not reach you.

Via consultants

1. Rejecting people recommended for interview without discussion with source.
2. Rejecting people from one agency on the basis of the agency description in favour of those from another agency, without testing a sample to see how the agencies' assessments stand up at interview.

The interview

1. Prevaricating over answers to legitimate candidate queries (we have even known this done about things which are a matter of public record).
2. Arriving late, drunk, sleepy, distraught, unbriefed or ill-tempered to the interview.
3. Using a substitute interviewer who is irrelevant, too senior or too inexperienced.
4. Failing to check by end of interview whether candidate is still interested.
5. Assuming consultant-introduced candidate is less satisfactory than direct candidate because the former asks fewer questions (but is in fact just better briefed).
6. Forgetting to mention that the beautiful bungalow offered has bullet-proof shutters – and why.
7. Passing secondhand or assumed data about local conditions – applies equally to Liverpool, Lerwick or Libya. The result is normally disastrous *after* hiring.
8. Describing conditions (bonus, holidays, etc.) without indicating company rules will defer or abbreviate them. Results in rejected offers or discontented employee.

Closing the sale

1. Assuming that, because candidates say they like you, the job and the company, they will wait indefinitely for an offer. (The best and the young are most at risk.)
2. Cold, stilted, formal offers lose candidates – often to inferior but more human ones! So do petty conditions. So do security-based requests for details of relatives – particularly if not explained.
3. Offers made without adequate thought or discussion about salary. Horribly common still on overseas jobs.

4. Getting huffy about post-offer queries.
5. Failing to check on work permits soon enough.
6. Recognising that an early candidate could do the job but waiting and hoping for more (either for comparison or marginal improvement). By the time you have rejected the later ones – or been rejected, the first bird has flown. Moral: ugly duckling in the hand is worth two hypothetical peacocks in the bush.

'You'll have to speak up, lad. There's a lot of background noise.'

Induction

Candidate arrives to find:

1. No room.
2. No desk, car, staff, work, etc.
3. No job! (or wrong title).
4. Predecessor still there, contrary to promise!
5. New boss/structure/location/parent company.
6. Nobody expecting them.
7. No pay (often follows 6).
8. No induction programme.
9. No company. . . .

Hiring for profit

People cost money. They should not be hired lightly. All too often hiring decisions are made without regard to the potential profit to be obtained from the performance of the job. Worse, the potential cost is often ignored.

For the first problem, the potential profit, good job analysis and a quick calculation should identify whether the results of the job are worth substantially more than the direct costs involved.

For the second, where nobody has bothered to think about profit and is not responsible for the expense (or accountable but irresponsible), in a normal, i.e. non-high-growth, business the appointment may well be unnecessary.

Taking a simple example, most organisations have several typists who may or may not be a pool but usually act like one to balance out overloads. (If they do not interact like this you have a different and worse problem, but curing it will also alleviate the need to hire or may even permit you to shed people.) Now or at some future date there is going to be pressure to hire an extra typist because 'There's too much work'. In a static business or a slow-growth one this statement is suspect.

On enquiry, you find one or more of the following to be causing the problem. All are readily soluble without the high cost of hiring an extra body.

1. Typists are being asked to do work outside their job descriptions.
2. They are choosing to do such work.
3. Internal memos which could be in manuscript are being typed.
4. Other internal forms, documents and reports which could be in manuscript are also being typed (adding to workload and the risk of error).
5. External documents which could be in manuscript without damaging the corporate image are being typed unnecessarily.
6. Private work is being done – usually but not always for management. You would be surprised how many otherwise responsible managers regard the free use of secretarial time and supplies on pet projects (charitable or otherwise) as an automatic perk of

their position. It is *very* bad for morale. Fortunately, because it is so damaging, typists usually find a way to bring it to the accidental attention of the manager's boss!

7. Repetitive typing is being done copy by copy, rather than on a word processor, memory typewriter, photocopier or other reproduction system. Memory typewriters are substantially cheaper than new staff, as indeed are many word processors. Some managers will defend this personalisation. On enquiry you will then find that so little thought has been given to the content of the document which needs to be personalised that it might as well be reproduced badly in blue duplicator ink on recycled paper for all the impact it is going to have. Managers who are not considerate of their staff often fail to consider their paperwork.

8. Some other traditional tasks have ceased to be necessary.

9. Users are not sharing the load. For example, the sort of manager who passes his outgoing mail back to be stuffed into envelopes after signing rather than stuffing one while reading the next one.

10. Chat. Gossip multiplies as the square of the number of people in a group. They do not even have to be in the same room but people will circulate until they have had their ration per capita.

These examples have been taken from the typing group, but a similar analysis of tasks will find duplicated or unnecessary work throughout the organisation.

Keeping people

Recruitment is expensive. Even if you reduce the direct costs to nil, which is sometimes feasible, the indirect costs and nuisance make it an unwelcome exercise if you are replacing someone competent. This alone can run into thousands of pounds. If the departing employee was making a worthwhile contribution to profit the true losses may be measured in tens of thousands.

There is an alternative. It is to try harder to keep people. Given a business with average staff tenure of five years, you can afford to spend up to one fifth of the average recruitment costs each year on a successful effort to keep good people. In extreme cases where the staff turnover in certain categories is worse than annual, the benefits of retention magnify accordingly, yet it is precisely this sort of organisation which is unhappy to spend money on people because they know the people will not be there next year. The few companies who try it reap massive benefits.

What can you spend the money on? Tactics and opinions will vary according to the business but you could consider:

1. More realistic salaries.
2. Loyalty bonuses, paid in arrears.
3. Training – not just in functional skills but in the wider aspects of the business so people feel more committed and have a better understanding of the contribution their jobs make and where they lead.
4. Profit sharing – on a real and open-ended formula which relates to the areas the beneficiaries can influence. There is nothing more damaging to morale than a company-wide scheme which yields poorly to people who know that their own profit centre has performed well as a result of exceptional personal efforts. They tend to take those personal efforts elsewhere, while the poor performers stay.
5. Find out why staff turnover is so high. The fact that it appears to be endemic in the sector does not mean it is incurable. Some incestuous sectors like the employment agency world of yesteryear accepted high staff turnover as a fact of life without exploring the reasons. The cause was a management style common to the eccentric entrepreneurs who headed a few of the key companies. Now that the sector has more professional managers and less proprietors in management the problem has reduced. Local research in your sector might well identify a similar factor x whose presence – or absence – is the cause of the trouble, no matter what the historic wisdom may suggest.
6. Being nicer to people. Just because certain categories of employee are invariably exceedingly bright, well-paid and in jobs which are inherently satisfying, because of the job interest and fulfilment attached to their tasks, there is no excuse for ignoring the wider aspects of motivation or supportive managerial behaviour.
7. Finally, a radical thought. In sectors where staff turnover is high there is a tendency for the hiring process to be less discriminating because the business needs the warm bodies to earn turnover. In fact the hiring process should be more selective than normal. It is exceptionally demotivating for good employees to be

surrounded by mediocrity, even if part of the manpower planning consists of firing the mediocre when they have proved their incompetence.

Candidates are customers

Once the decision to hire has been taken, the company must take particular care in its attitude to candidates. Though this applies to every outside contact, candidates are the most throughly abused class and become a prime example.

The problem is that most managers, including personnel managers, regard candidates for jobs at all levels as cannon fodder. They forget to treat them as they would wish to be treated in similar circumstances. Sometimes this results from incompetence, sometimes from lack of thought, sometimes from a deliberate and quite counter-productive ego-trip.

The reasons are less important than the results. Candidates who have been badly treated become illwill ambassadors for the company. They stop being potential employees. They stop their friends becoming potential employees. They do not become customers. They make life harder for you when they are later working for key suppliers. Very few bad interviewers or apathetic personnel staff think about this.

The lesson has much wider application to outside contacts, beyond the obvious examples of customers and suppliers. Your professional advisers may also feel the same way if messed about. Telephone callers who suffer incompetent or surly responses will feel ill-used. Even drivers carved up by one of your vans may not feel too happy. If you care about your corporate image, take a look at your procedures for dealing with the world at large. Start with candidates and you may get a nasty shock.

Signing on

Several booklets and numerous chapters have been written about training new employees, but guidance to employees themselves is much more limited and usually assumes that the best action is merely a mirror image of corporate behaviour. This is seldom valid. Even companies with first-rate training schemes for new shopfloor employees are deficient in handling management level arrivals. New employees have to compensate for their defects, and go beyond anything the employer can do, in formulating their own programme. The following section is written for the new arrival, but the lessons could help the new arrival's guides and mentors.

If you are ambitious, or even if you are not and just seek to adopt a low profile for a quiet life, there is much you should be doing for your own benefit as a new employee and for that of your new employer. The things to do, appear to do, fail to do and choose not to do in the first few weeks in a new job can affect your career in that organisation and beyond it. There is also action to be taken before you arrive, from the moment you take the decision to accept a future employer's offer.

Some companies may give you a briefing pack. Hopefully this would include product literature, potted company history, employee's guide to the location you are to join and a company handbook, if one exists. You already have the job description and annual report you obtained at interview, we hope. If you don't get any of these things – ask the company or gather them informally. Also check whether anyone has written a book about the company. Any book helps. The range includes the classic 'This is what we've done for the last 50/100/200 years' type (specially commissioned for the anniversary celebrations and now out of print) at one end and a searing denunciation of the capitalist/racist/fascist/bourgeois/reactionary/polluting/monopolist oppressors at the other. In between there are some well-balanced pop paperbacks about big companies, major takeover or specialist sectors (motor, property and so on) which are extremely revealing to new employees. Instead of spending the first six months wondering how Ron survived the takeover or why nobody pays any attention to Sir Frederick you can play the correct politics from day one. Any company more than fifty years old must have a company history book or booklet somewhere. Boards cannot resist the urge to write (or commission) them as the jubilee is reached. Finally, before arriving you should if possible lay hands on a set of organisation charts in order to see where you are to fit in the company's operation.

Any company more than 50 years old must have a company history.

This preparation reduces the chances that you will be floundering for your first few weeks. The first few days of meeting people may also be easier if you have some prior knowledge of the key names and jobs. The impression you create will be improved if you have obviously done your homework properly and first impressions are just as important as later performance.

The first few days should also include a lot of paper and information gathering. Quietly identify all the manuals, procedures, standing instructions and even statutory instruments affecting your areas and take a preliminary glance at them. Ask intelligent questions wherever you go – people expect it and it helps them to direct their briefing efforts. Find how your cost centre allocation works. Also find how to charge things to other cost centres, legally. Make friends with the secretarial and clerical staff and the key support people like telephonist, receptionist, stationery manager and janitor. Take advice from the secretary on all matters of self-interest (anything you want to know that might sound petty or grasping if put to your superiors). By all means let people volunteer information on known office problems, but take them without undue comment.

Learn also any unwritten rules, customs and idiosyncracies that do not get in the rule book. For example 'don't wear suede shoes if you're meeting Sir William', or 'you can park anywhere in the managers' car park, we're so democratic, except of course in space seventeen, that's the Old Man's'.

Beware of people who seem over eager to make friends. They may have been rejected by everyone else. Equally, do not be put off by people who are cool initially but do check whether your arrival has created political problems for them. You may have to do some remedial work to rebuild other people's images before you can get a reasonable working relationship. Also beware of reproducing the social patterns of your previous company without prior observation. If you lunch with the 'wrong' people, or in the 'wrong' place, or socialise with your secretary, it can be doomladen in spite of the fact that parallel examples were considered democratic and to be encouraged in the old firm. Most important, do not talk too much about the old firm, for any reason.

The point about observation is also crucial. Much of the information you are gathering may tempt you to volunteer adverse criticism of systems, or the lack of systems, which appear quite intolerably inefficient by contrast with things you have been used to. In the process of reading your staff's job descriptions and your own you may find glaring omissions or unnecessary work. Show absorption and minimum comment. A few weeks' quiet observation may demonstrate:

1. That the system you dislike is actually the pet project of one of your superiors, in which case you will have to tread very warily.
2. There is a good reason for the anomalies and they constitute a worthwhile compromise.
3. Your staff want to change them too and are straining at the leash to be given the chance.
4. Changes would be opposed from *below* unless you do your marketing properly.

Only after this is it advisable to start changing things, when you have learned the basic routines and established how much change can be achieved without treading on toes outside your own area. Nevertheless, it is very important that your programme of review and criticism starts on day one, before you become inured to the most glaring faults.

To sum up, there are nine golden rules for new arrivals:

1. DO keep good time in the first few months and leave your personal flexitime till much later.
2. DO retain the image you presented at interview and avoid contradicting anything you may have said then.
3. DO remember and build on the things you were told at interview – names, facts, problems, even problem people.
4. DO make sure the company's solvent, as soon as possible.
5. DO talk to personnel staff, your superior or your predecessor to get a brief on current personal or work problems of your staff.
6. DO give your secretary opportunities to shine in month one and DON'T take away all the new found chances when you have learned how things work.
7. DON'T make gratuitous contact with top management until there is something worthwhile to talk about.
8. DON'T make arbitrary judgements about even the worst staff around you. They may have hidden merits.
9. DON'T let the person inducting you introduce you to too many people at once. You risk forgetting their names while they remember yours.

Success through succession

Once installed, it is surprising how few people bother to consider and plan their short-term progress. Even those who have a grand design directed towards public company directorship at an early age fail to consider the variables which affect their rise within a company.

This is not talking just about getting one's boss's job, but about regrading, 'diagonal' promotions and other increases in responsibilities. In practice, promotion is the most significant. The requirements for advancement are fairly simple. There must be a historic vacancy or a need for a new job. One must be eligible for that vacancy in terms of personality, performance, technical relevance and managerial expertise. There must be an internal development scheme which permits one to be considered (for those in administrative, finance or personnel roles one can often get such a scheme introduced if none exists – given time and persuasion). There must be no danger that one is indispensable in one's present job – hence one needs a successor.

Learn also any unwritten rules.

Taking these requirements one by one, it is obvious that some of them are beyond one's control. However, none of them are totally beyond influence. A vacancy can be created by assisting one's immediate superior to get promoted, by presenting a case for a new function or a separation of existing functions or by getting one's boss fired or demoted.

One's eligibility is more complex. It is fairly easy to be technically relevant for part of the job above one, if not all of it, but the management style has to change as one goes up the ladder. My personal preference is for doing any job in the most relaxed and indeed light-hearted way possible, but this is certainly not the ideal style to encourage promotion. A crisp and dynamic facade, suggesting

28

hidden depths, top management potential and a healthy sporting outlook, may be nearer the mark.

Widening one's eligibility is much more helpful. Unless one is right at the top of a fairly narrow pyramid, there may be positions ranking above you in related specialist areas to which you can make a diagonal move. This also avoids the special problems of promotion within a department. To be considered for such diagonal promotions you need to have evinced strong and continuing interest in the work of the areas concerned, coupled with prompt cooperation on all matters of joint concern. This is of course speculative but has other benefits unconnected with promotion.

The need to have an identifiable successor is in some ways the most difficult task of all, particularly if you have already been rushed up the managerial ladder at an above average rate. It becomes rather like a game of chess where you are obliged to think n moves ahead so that everyone's successor has a successor. Given that this is necessary, you then have to consider who in the chain needs development most. Do you send your own developing subordinate on a training course – or go yourself – or persuade your boss to go? The permutations are many, the politics Machiavellian.

Creating a candidate for your own job also runs you into danger. If promotion doesn't come in time, they may be good enough to get a better job outside. Hence a need for not one but two potential climbers. Intelligent delegation, one of the best ways to develop people, may also work you out of a job unless your own superior is delegating equally furiously.

Perhaps it is not so surprising after all that some people forget the whole idea of short-term career planning. Luck and hard work can do remarkably well.

Directorship delusion

Assuming that either by careful planning or luck, or a combined effort, steady progress is made up the managerial ladder, there are far too many rational, reasonable, logical people around who go silly at the idea of a board appointment. Other things being equal, provided you have the power and money appropriate to the job, there are considerable merits in not being a director. Working directorships are often offered for the wrong reasons. Most of those who seek fulltime directorships do so for misguided motives.

The requirements for advancement are fairly simple . . .

Consider the good reasons for appointing anyone a director. From the company's point of view, it may improve a person's capacity to negotiate with the outside world. In a public company the presence of more than the statutory minimum board may be comforting to investors, brokers and the press. Additionally, if the company has always had directors at the head of a particular function, the title may add to the individual's stature within the organisation.

There are no good reasons for most people, thinking of their own interests, to seek or accept fulltime directorships. Personal vanity is not a good reason. Custom is not. The presence of a director's title on one's career record is illusory in most cases (excluding non-executive appointments, which have certain merits). Trying to get a non-board post in another company is actually easier if you are *not* a director of your present company than if you are, and the harsh fact is that most fulltime board appointments are made from within the company concerned. Thus only a minority will come onto the open market, to be filled through advertisements, or search and selection consultants. These will tend to be filled on merit, not on an accident of title and more attention should always be paid to job content than job title.

The final argument is the immense burden of statutory responsibility a director shoulders. Other things being equal directors do not add to their power at the same time as they accept this burden. The level of influence of a senior management team depends more on their joint and several personalities and powers of argument than on their directorships. Strong MDs will do what they want, subject to the quality of opposition or persuasion around them, not other people's titles. If directors disagree violently with any policy there is an extra problem. The obligation to resign is rather greater for a dissenting director than for a manager. Think about directors' responsibilities. The list is horrifying. They allow individuals to put a noose around their neck along with the title; the sins and omissions of colleagues and predecessors twitching the rope from day one.

It is probably better to resign than be sacked. There are exceptions. If you are fighting a major point of principle, with statutes on your side, and your work record is otherwise clean, it may be reasonable to say 'Do it my way or fire me'. If they do fire you, you may have a classic case of wrongful dismissal. If they do it the right way, you have either acquired a breathing space in which to find a more honourable job, or, if you want to stay, may have established a powerful precedent.

The most important budget

The next section of this book will look at a variety of management approaches to financial decision-making, but first we might consider this in relation to good personnel management. Even the best managers often ignore the necessity for supporting the personnel department and the necessity for involving oneself in the motivation of staff, financially and otherwise.

Managers in almost any size of company have an obligation to aid and comfort the personnel department, a department which is generally not as articulate as it might be in fighting for its rights. The personnel budget should be one of the links between managers and personnel staff, not one of the barriers. Personnel budget here does not mean just the headcount budget but the total expenditure on bodies, companywide, and on all personnel and related services. Usually the status of the personnel function is less than it deserves. It is unrealistic for other managers to sit back and accept this as recognition of their own superiority. Both the ranking and remuneration of the personnel staff should be such that you have above average people in the function. Only when this happens will the company have a really satisfactory support service. Satisfactory in this context also means cost effective. This has to be the ultimate justification of all personnel work to the shareholders and general management. All personnel work can and should be quantified and sold to the board.

Management is generally hopelessly unaware of the true cost and value of the recruitment, conditioning, training, development and retention of personnel, at all levels. Personnel staff, embroiled in their crises on each of these fronts, can fail to cost or disclose the damage because of the implied reflection on their past work. The financial manager can be more impartial.

The costs of staff and labour turnover are seldom the subject of regular reporting, yet they are shatteringly significant. Very few companies seriously weigh the cost of recruitment against the cost of retention. In crude terms, if you fail to pay a £20,000 employee the 15% increment they warrant against the 10% you think you can afford, you have a good chance of losing out in three respects. Not only will you have to spend £2,000–£4,000 to replace them, but you will also suffer the reduced working contribution of a new person running at part efficiency. Worse, you'll have to buy the new one at the market rate, which may equal or exceed the figure you should have paid in the first place. You have saved £1,000 for three months (say £250) and suffered up to £10,000 direct costs and inefficiency. Far better to keep above average people by paying them realistically above average salaries. This leads one to the argument which financial managers should encourage in staffing battles = it is cheaper to have four excellent staff of a particular type at say £15,000, rather than five less good at

£12,000. For one thing, they generate less in other overheads; for another, if one wants to be cynical, if they each spend two hours a week talking to each of the others, you only lose twelve working hours rather than twenty. There are of course quality benefits too.

This brings us to headcount or manpower budgets. These are typically American, but none the worse for that. People form a very large part of an organisation's expenses and their activity varies to some extent with the volume of business. They also generate other indirect expenses in a fairly precise progression. The national economy might be in a happier state if it had been recognised years ago that companies without a headcount budget and the willingness to apply it as a cost-reduction tool in times of stress are doing less than justice to their shareholders. It is possible that the unemployment problem might also be better now if the rethinking which this philosophy demands had also been done years ago.

Investment analysts in the press draw unhappy comparisons between the labour utilisation of various groups. They are particularly fond of doing this between particular motor manufacturers or between Britain and, say, West Germany. The industrial manager should where possible be making comparisons of personnel costs with other companies in the same industry. It is often said that adequate figures are not available. Rubbish. They may not be a matter of public record, but it is usually possible to find a source without damaging your own or anyone else's professional ethics. Too precise a comparison will be meaningless because of the different methods of cost allocation from company to company, but a general comparison should identify the more dramatic inefficiencies.

This raises another contentious point. There is a case for allocating the costs of personnel recruitment and training to each user department, but this can lead to a reduction in cooperation with the personnel staff because each department feels its own budget performance will be adversely affected. On balance, allocations of this kind are probably inadvisable.

Secretaries

One final point about the right people; a secretary is often the yardstick by which a manager is judged, far more than most people round about realise. Managers should recognise this and act accordingly. Because of the historic imbalance of opportunity against secretarial staff in most businesses, it is entirely possible that the IQ of the average secretary exceeds the IQ of the boss. The thoughtful manager will take advantage of this rather than be frightened. With practice, much of any manager's job can be delegated, not least because very few managers can or should write or dictate enough to occupy more than a fragment of a secretary's time typing.

There is another bonus. The secretarial network is often much more powerful and effective than the managerial net, so that tasks delegated to the secretary get done without overt conflict, when managerial communication would be ineffective or counter-productive. Anything which allows the secretary to move away from the typewriter and onto key tasks will benefit the manager as manager, trainer and shining example.

It is entirely possible that the IQ of the average secretary exceed the IQ of the boss.

34

3
Making money

Profitable employment

Have you reviewed your Job Description lately? It may have a glaring omission. Every job example should start with these words, or a paraphrase of them: 'The primary responsibility and duty of the employee is to maximise the profitability and efficiency of the company'. Only then can one go on to mundane detail: 'As a means to this end, this employee will be particularly involved in costing, etc. . . .'

There is no automatic merit in insuring safety, solvency, continuity of employment, continuity of the company, good industrial relations, provision of a good service to customers, good products, good management information and compliance with the law. They are only justified as a means to the stated end.

But the means are more visible and often become more important than the end. A walk through most urban streets will prove this. You are almost certain to find, in any group of shops more than thirty years old, a small trader who would profit more from selling the freehold or leasehold and reinvesting than from continuing to trade.

The shareholders of a motor manufacturer should not give a damn about maintaining the company's market penetration unless that in itself is inexorably linked to improved profitability (and it is not). Solvency is useful, but not an end in itself. If one looks behind the problem, liquidation may be preferable to injections of capital. Good industrial relations are useful, but a therapeutic strike may be better when you are overstocked with finished products! Forward planning may be meaningless and costly in a business where the forward markets themselves are guesswork.

These are extremes and their logical extension would be to eliminate all non-essentials and end up with a service business with a very small staff, no fixed assets, no products, no inventory, no labour force and a capacity for profit growth disproportionate to its turnover or employment of resources and people. (It's called selection consultancy, by the way.) However, a more common example is the manufacturer who can accept the wisdom of sourcing component supplies outside the company, but still does not consider whether to subcontract all the productive processes and concentrate on marketing the finished product or factoring someone else's product.

There is room for the principle – of working for profit without traditional constraints – to be applied by most of us. So many good ideas at management meetings end on the scrapheap when they threaten some entrenched doctrine within the company. Entrenched doctrines are often obsolete. They need to be taken out and examined critically from time to time. Every so often the trench can usefully be a grave. Consider how your organisation's job descriptions would look if the necessity of corporate profit became the prime target of each one.

Revealing all

Looking behind the profit at the facts and figures which create it, and continuing the theme of learning from others' mistakes, it is constructive to consider some of the information usually left out of a company's annual report. Facts and figures, in particular certain key ratios, which would be useful to shareholders and managers alike. The obvious ones would be on capital gearing, liquidity, utilisation of capital, stock turnover, debtor turnover and return on assets. Most of these can be derived from the annual report and accounts but it seems desirable that they should be spelt out more explicitly.

One should be entitled to know which members of a board are fulltime, which parttime and which are totally non-executive (attending board . meetings only). Their professional qualifications would also be of interest. Declaration of directors' benefits could also be salutary. How many use company flats, houses, cars or aeroplanes? And how many company cars are there, in all? How many units of real property? (Shareholders and managers should know to what extent they are accidentally investing in property rather than the company's primary activities. Balance sheet values are only part of the picture.) Some other questions deserve to be answered as a matter of course, although not all are to do with ratios:

1. How much expenditure was disallowed for tax purposes and, where it is significant, why?
2. How does the company's average yield compare with that to be obtained in the money market in the period?
3. How does its share price movement compare with the FT index? (overall and perhaps for its sector).
4. Average salary per employee *v* national average wage (and *v* known competitors, perhaps).
5. Turnover and net profit per employee.
6. Percentage of turnover generated by top 10% of company's customers?
7. The reasons why debtors exceed the theoretical level appropriate to the company's official terms of credit and the amount involved.
8. Historic 'growth' record adjusted for the value of the pound.

There are certain other points which one could not safely insist that a management disclose to the outside world, but it would be salutary to insist both that top management were provided with the data, and that the auditors verified its accuracy. For example, perhaps directors ought to be compelled to be aware of the following:

1. Basic ratios of chief competitors.
2. Dependence on key parts suppliers.
3. Dependence on key customers.
4. Market penetration, if their markets have finite sizes.
5. Whether the shareholders would have done better to invest in cash, gold or sardines one, five and ten years ago? (This will not make the directors better managers but it concentrates the mind wonderfully.)

The vertical transmission of information and commands is one of the biggest causes of self-generated unproductive work in British business. Just take a staff situation in which a Chairman requests data from an MD. The request goes to the specialist Director and could then go to the Financial Controller, Assistant Controller, specialist manager, specialist supervisor, section leader and finally to the relevant analyst. The time and effort involved in transmitting the request and replying can exceed the value of the data and the risk of errors in transmission is high. (The chain described above is brief by comparison with one which involves divisional and sub-group staffs!).

While we consider disciplines of this sort we may as well consider the balloon game. Directors should be forced to consider at regular intervals which of their company's activities they can best afford to lose, why they have chosen not to lose it, and how they propose to make it more worthwhile in the future. Hopefully this would have one of three results:

1. They sell or close the operation and apply the resources elsewhere.
2. They make it more efficient or otherwise less dispensable.
3. The process of analysis makes them realise the operation is more necessary or more profitable than it had been assumed.

The penetration obsession

Some of the best managers are obsessed with market penetration. They know the size of the market for their products. They know their penetration of that market. Sometimes they know their competitors' figures too. Bully for them. This makes for very sophisticated analysis of their market performance and a feeling of awareness and control. Rather like having accurate instruments at 70 mph on a foggy motorway.

Sales staff often imply that the need to increase sales in a fairly finite market is their biggest problem. Problem it may be, but it is not a valid objective. Increased profit is an acceptable objective, but increased sales and market penetration are not essential routes towards it. They are actually very dangerous, because competitors notice and react, with sales effort, other marketing action, price wars and 'dirty tricks' of their own. Why not leave them in peace? There are alternative routes to profit. In particular, you can expand the market and keep the extra bit all to yourself. Your colleagues may have done it already without realising its tactical significance in a competitive market. There are three clear cases:

Directors should be forced to consider at regular intervals which of their company's activities they can best afford to lose.

1. Sell to people who didn't buy the product or service before.
2. Export more.
3. Sell to people for whom these purchases are not identified as part of the official market, or sell a product derivative which is not part of the traditional market statistics.

It may be important that you avoid action which expands the market for you and your competitors. This may make marginal competitors viable or give them by accident a core of profitable business which enables them to compete more effectively with you in areas where you hold market leadership. The need to consider whether your marketing action is creating an expanded total market is vital – and seldom appreciated. Unless you are in a sector where you and your competitors are prepared to band together to increase public awareness of the sector as a whole, helping your competitors by accident seldom makes sense.

Price resistance

Pricing is a blind spot for many managers, financial and other. Most are scared of their sales colleagues and their view of the price sensitivity of the market. In consequence, the sales preference for the status quo often prevails. Even in static conditions this would be unfortunate. In times of inflation it can be disastrous.

Finance staff normally want to increase prices and sales staff say that this is not possible because key accounts will be lost. Usually both sides are right. A few key accounts will be lost, but if they were really so price sensitive they were probably on special terms already, making them highly marginal in profit terms. The only reason the sales staff knew they were price sensitive was their past negotiation for special prices, deals, discounts or payment terms.

Getting back to basics, the managers' role in an organisation is to generate the maximum profit for the shareholders, now and for the future. There is no obligation to price at a level which maximises production, unless it can also be shown to maximise current and medium term profits.

Many managers imagine that they have been involved in product pricing exercises when they have merely been:
1. Defending arbitrary gross margin levels.
2. Resisting marketing staff price-cutting proposals, on the assumption that sales and marketing staff are always wrong.
3. Pricing against alleged competitors whose products are not wholly or even partially competitive.

Pricing decisions must overcome corporate infighting. We must concentrate on the principles and common mistakes.

Significant factors affecting pricing decisions include:
1. capacity available;

2. product costs (variable and semi-variable);
3. competitors' prices;
4. competitors' market acceptance;
5. existing market shares;
6. market needs in terms of quality, reliability and other non-financial factors.

Most of these factors are often ignored or their relevance obscured by subjective judgements. It should be self-evident that the best price structure for a group of products is that which generates the best corporate net profit. Often the sales staff are concerned to defend turnover above all else. Being market leader on turnover is very exciting. It also leaves room for someone else to run second or third on turnover and come first on profit. There are no prizes for guessing which company is more highly valued or more likely to survive in adverse conditions.

The pitfalls are not always obvious. They include:

1. underpricing, to maximise turnover, too often done when true gross margins are dangerously low. This is often achieved by a failure to identify all variable and semi-variable costs generated by extra volume;
2. underpricing by failing to take note of value advantages over a competitor's similar but inferior product;
3. overpricing where gross margins are high and there really is some price sensitivity, thus underutilising capacity;
4. underpricing one product to support an associated one – occasionally logical but seldom properly thought through and thus often insupportable;
5. giving attention to price rather than improving the product or service, which would eliminate price sensitivity – there being many markets where performance is paramount.

All these errors can be identified by a few hours' study in the High Street. There may be a few examples lurking in your company price structure as well. For those who wish to do something about the matter the theorists' 'price elasticity curve' may come to mind as a useful tool.

There is a related practical graphic aid where existing products are involved. Statisticians may have a better word for it; it could be called a 'profit vulnerability graph', and it is arrived at by plotting one curve representing those combinations of volume and unit price which would produce the same total gross profit per annum for that product. On this can be superimposed a second curve representing informed estimates of probable volumes at particular prices. Any sector where the latter 'probable' volumes significantly exceed the 'necessary' volumes for profit maintenance may be considered to indicate a safe area for price movement, which may be upward or downward. Before getting too euphoric about the opportunities it is as well to indicate a cut-off point for known capacity limits, although projection beyond this may in some cases appear to justify an increase in plant capacity.

Paying compensation

In credit management it is customary to undertake a regular review of existing customers and quietly eliminate the ones who will not pay their accounts within a reasonable time. You can find examples of this in companies of all sizes and types. It is of course true that the threat of discontinued supply sometimes makes these customers mend their ways. However, others do not and the sanction is applied.

There is a case for being nice to the difficult customer. In many businesses the gross margins are good and the competition fierce so that you ought to be collecting customers like this, at very firm prices, and planning to supply them at extended terms (without telling them). The result will be that you suffer a little loss on the extended credit, make a large profit on the sale, keep the customer for next time and retain or improve your market penetration.

This is not quite as simple as it sounds. You have to be sure that customers are really solvent and are just taking extended credit as part of their way of life, not because they are trading themselves into the ground. You also have to direct your sales force carefully so that their tactics do not run counter to yours. This is not difficult; sales staff prefer to keep on selling, even when accounts are overdue. The knowledge that they are permitted to do it and that they have a tactical advantage will revive them. The theory has wider applications. Being nice to the difficult supplier, customer, or client may make you the only people in town for whom they retain warm feelings. There have been many occasions when we have been nice to the most outrageously offensive clients to find later that we have earned goodwill when all around were allowing their naked emotions to show through. We got new business as a result, and they turned out in nearly every case to be quite worthwhile.

Growing pains

Acquisitions are the purchase of another business, company, firm or its essential assets, rights, patents, tools and trademarks, etc. They are seductive. Some acquisitions bring some of the benefits expected, they all bring unexpected penalties. The 'urge to merge' should be countered with some less emotive considerations:

1. The cost of investigating even the abortive ones is considerable, whether measured in external fees or internal management time. It will also come as no surprise that you reject some because they do not fit your corporate plan, although you should have known that before you started the exercise.
2. The short term cash flow is almost invariably worse than forecast.
3. Unexpected losses exceed unexpected profit items.
4. The problems of integration are always underestimated.
5. The people you want leave and the bad ones stay.
6. Anomalies between the two sets of employee benefits pose IR problems and add costs.
7. Shareholders, press and Stock Exchange usually misunderstand.
8. So do the unions.
9. Nobody considers the tax implications early enough.
10. There is a temptation to keep unnecessary staff.
11. In its effect on sales, the whole is often less than the sum of the parts.
12. The problems of greater scale may exceed the benefits.

There may be credible alternatives to growth by acquisition:

1. Investment in organic growth.
2. Organic growth without investment.
3. Leave the money in the money market.
4. Make existing operations more efficient.
5. Make 'new' products under licence.
6. Buy the rights to someone else's invention.
7. Lean on your own R and D function.

The question to ask is always: 'What is the best strategy other than this acquisition and how does it compare financially?'.

Keeping the company doctor away

Contrasting with the desire to grow is the situation which demands a company doctor. 'Company doctors' exist for a variety of reasons. They would be largely unnecessary if there were enough good managers doing their own jobs properly. The reasons they are required normally boil down to:

1. Critical cash situation.
2. Critical profit situation.
3. Necessity for restructuring or rationalisation, often in the wake of a bid or to forestall future bids.

Most of the things which have to be done in these circumstances would have been done anyway by a profit-motivated board adequately advised by a competent and forceful financial director. The variables which have created the problem probably include the attitude of the board, the inadequacy and inaccuracy of the management information, the strength of character of the senior finance manager and the incredible collective reluctance of many managers to take unpleasant decisions.

Some of these are curable, in particular the management information problem. Less obviously, the problem of the financial manager's impact. Intelligent and strong financial management is the cure to keep away the company doctor. Going through the common factors of company 'medical practice' it becomes evident how much is really in the financial manager's hands.

In an emergency, remaining solvent and improving the cash flow position is actually even more urgent than improving profitability. Reducing stock and debtors, fighting off creditors, gaining the cooperation of the company's banker(s), nearly all fall squarely in the finance manager's court. Improved credit control and restrictions on purchasing authorities will solve some of the short term difficulties. Backlogs in the personal ledgers, however slight, can affect the cash flow disproportionately. Invoices or statements which go out on

Friday instead of the next Monday might improve the cash position by 1% of turnover. Think what a week can do. The medium term things which go to improve cash flow should also have been identified earlier by intelligent financial analysis.

The sale of real property or other major fixed assets (or sale and leaseback) stems quite logically from the fact that people are not in business to own things but to use them for profit. Broadly, this only ceases to apply when revenue expenses associated with leasing or hiring exceed the cost of the investment necessary to own. With property values moving as they have recently, a regular review of this balance is essential even for fairly short leaseholds. For instance, it is no good saying that a separate geographical unit, also a separate profit-centre, is making £10,000 a year pre-tax profit and 25% RoA when the rent of the site is at an archaic £2,000 instead of its current realistic rental of £12,000. Many managements won't make this comparison unless their financial managers force them to it.

If attention of this sort to current and fixed assets still does not solve the problem, it may be logical to consider factoring, invoice discounting or a revolving acceptance credit facility, always assuming that your returns on the incremental monies made available more than cover the cost of these facilities. Nothing in this list is beyond the wit of the average financial manager.

However, when we consider the other half of the company doctor's work, financial managers are as dependent on influencing others as on action within their own sphere of operations. The aim is to render all aspects of the business genuinely and adequately profitable, or to dispose of the bits which cannot be turned round. All this must be achieved while retaining the people, sales and supplies essential to the continuing operations. It may also involve quite a lot of creative work, making sure you have enough information to identify accurately the unprofitable elements. The items starred on the chart below are within the control of the finance staff. The remainder deserve, indeed demand, indirect pressure on specialist management and the board.

When a company finds itself unable to meet its liabilities, it is important that there should be a first 'flash report' on the business and an assessment of its asset situation and, particularly, its profit potential. There must be good solicitors to deal with difficult creditors, and creditors must realise that a receiver is just around the corner. There is logic in prompt, frank disclosure and prompt token payments to creditors. One could also advise against excessively brutal attacks on overheads, because the company needs to make profits after it has paid back creditors, so some continued expenditure on advertising and marketing is essential.

Profit Improvement

Increase Revenue

Increase Volume	Increase Margins	Other
New products?	*Review discount structures	*Minimise tax
Better marketing	Pricing action	Maximise recovery from government grants, etc.
Better sales incentives		*Maximise interest on cash, short term deposits, etc.
Remove capacity bottlenecks		
*Pricing action?		

Reduce Costs

Reduce Direct Costs	Reduce Overheads
Improve labour efficiency	*Locate and fire surplus staff and indirect labour
Reduce material waste	*Cut advertising, PR, marketing, research, other outside services
Reduce material prices	Consider using smaller premises
Value analysis	Control purchases of indirect materials
	*Review costs of distribution and handling
	*Minimise borrowing costs
	*Minimise reporting systems?

Equally there is a case for paying key employees more! A carrot from the phoenix may be appropriate. In any case, it is important to build up the confidence of the existing staff who should share in or even monopolise the credit for improvements. On a more pessimistic note, the company doctor and indeed all professional advisers will need to ensure that they are paid virtually on a cash basis – at least monthly in any case – and be prepared to get a receiver appointed if things go wrong. They should not let emotions overcome professional training and instinct. Too many reputations have been lost by those who let personal pride in their rescue capacity get in the way of commercial prudence or risk assessment.

Management in adversity

Adverse conditions have merits; they demand and enforce management action in a way favourable circumstances never can. Ideally, the threat of adversity should be enough. As a catalyst, its imminence is just as good as its presence, provided somebody notices the threat (in many companies they may not). Most managers are readily seduced by the trivia of day-to-day affairs. At least, if adversity is lurking in the wings, we can use it constructively.

It should be self-evident that even the most average of managers when ruin is staring them all in the face, are better motivated to:
– concentrate
– pull together
– abjure politics
– assess priorities
– identify key objectives
– make sacrifices
– sweep aside trivia
– make unpleasant decisions.

This presupposes that they don't panic. For management by, with, during and in spite of panic, see the next section.

If you accept the basic premise, you may contend that there isn't enough adversity around in your particular environment to stir even the most twitchy manager to action. But you can create a threat of adversity as a tactical weapon in your management armoury, or focus attention on a real micro-problem which is going to be macro if someone doesn't act.

You can create a threat of adversity . . .

One particularly bright pair of operators in the Ford Dealer Development team in the 1960s found the slow decision-making process irritating and evolved what for our purposes we can call the DD system. This short cut circumvented all the normal channels, all the normal lead times and all the normal approvals.

It consisted of waiting until the last forty-eight hours before a decision was needed, having checked that key UK signatories were available, and then rushing the project round the head office with shrill cries (varied for each occasion) of 'if we don't get approval by tomorrow, we'll lose the deal because:

– Chrysler wants the dealership
– they'll go bust
– the owner's dying

– a property company wants the site
– the sky will fall on our heads'
and so on.

This process was not only remarkably successful but it saved the DD team from a lot of unnecessary paperwork and justifications. One of its key features, apart from its flagrant abuse of the system, was its seductive appeal to senior managers, whose adrenalin flowed in a way it never could using 'conventional channels'. They were actually needed. Today! Now! Their day was justified. They had 'thought on their feet' and done something specific for the common good. Even the obstructive, indecisive people who demanded total information before making each normal non-decision were seduced into signatures, clucking nervously but signing nevertheless. Avoiding a US counter-signature also gave satisfaction.

The same principle applied to pricing. The managers who would take weeks to consider (and lose) a new fleet order with an unusual price structure were trampled underfoot when a harsh cruel market in the mid 1960s presented us with the distinct possibility of:

– short time working
– industrial unrest
– losing skilled labour.

Faced with this particular piece of adversity the board had no difficulty approving a proposal to sell vans to the Post Office at only four shillings (20p) per unit more than the direct cost of making them. As a result, BMC went on short time instead.

This sort of attitude can work wonders in union relations as well. Union officials, shop stewards and their members are not stupid. Most of them are realists. When the choice is between unpalatable economies and total disaster, reason usually prevails but the danger has to be evident and credible. If managements fail to communicate the problems clearly, the 'adversity bonus' fails to operate.

The principle has wider application. The ingenuity and cooperation engendered by:

– strikes
– hot competition

– receivership
– imminent take over
– cash flow crises
– fire or flood
– three day week

all prove the point, so even if you cannot burn the plant down, there must be an equivalent plot in your locker somewhere.

Panic

Panic is an excellent incentive to action. Be prepared to take advantage of it if others can be relied on to help. Your primary task as a good manager should be to analyse the problem while all about you are headless chickens, and call them to order when you have a convincing explanation, solution or palliative.

Given that you are planning for what may be a fairly mediocre peer group, they probably have other defects in their handling of the business. Do consider whether, as the waves of terror wash over them, and you offer them salvation, you might also sneak into the package some pet project which their reactionary attitudes would otherwise have stifled.

Panics are like cocktail parties. Nobody remembers what anybody said, the morning after. Make good use of their oblivion.

Overdoing it

When confronted with a problem there is a natural tendency to take too much action, thereby overcompensating. Examples are rife. Take the conventional solution of the company which is not selling as much of a particular product as it should be. Very crudely, it could:

1. Take pricing action.
2. Take product action.
3. Improve its marketing.

Few managements can resist the temptation to do two or even three of these, rather than the really relevant one. The probable results may well include a profit improvement, but they will also include unnecessary costs and/or a sacrifice of gross revenue, which could have been avoided.

Even single actions can constitute overcorrection in this context. For example, if one is firing at a target and one's first shot is just outside the bull's-eye, there is a temptation to correct one's aim on the next shot, without considering whether the error falls into the likely pattern of deviation to be expected of even the most perfect rifle at that distance. The apparently logical correction is thus likely to be overcorrection.

Remember how British Rail, faced with the choice of cutting services or raising prices, normally does both, thereby precipitating a repeat disaster? Remember how Civil and Armed Service budgets used to be based on the previous year's actuals, so that if you were economical one year you were deprived the next? Avoid unnecessary action and you will find more time to plan what you do do. Or you may prove you are redundant.

'This is serious Carruthers. Who failed to drink the regulation 9.7 cups of tea per day last year?'

Needs mustn't

Projects based on necessity are usually suspect. With all other justifications you can consider alternative objectives and alternative means, but where 'we must have it' reason flies out of the window. Good managers should grit their teeth, dig their heels in and demand alternatives even if the closure of a plant or the death of a product line is the result. If these alternatives are not considered and evaluated we have management by crisis rather than by reason.

It is bad enough to be prevented from doing nothing. What is worse is to be disqualified from considering more constructive alternatives in a reasonable and more leisurely time frame.

Best practice

If there are reservations about capital projects based on 'necessity', there is a similar problem about all expenditure based on the alleged objective of 'best modern practice'.

Using 'best practice' as the primary justification for anything is cheating. It is not a valid objective. Every time we introduce criteria unrelated to profit, but hinting slyly at excellence and massaging corporate and personal vanities, we do a disservice to ourselves and our colleagues. All decisions should be justifiable in financial terms.

This does not imply fighting for 'worst practice', but the disciples of good practice should think through their reasons for recommending it. What is the cost of not doing it? Why? What are the risks?

All being well, best practice should win most of the time, but two extra benefits will emerge from the discipline of fuller justification. The first is that at some time in the next year or so, someone will discover that 'best practice' in something isn't actually worth it – or isn't actually best. The second, perhaps more important, is that the big spenders who have been quietly collecting approvals for their pet schemes on the grounds that 'it's best practice', 'it's essential' or 'everybody's doing it' will have to go away and construct a better case for them. When they can and get used to doing so, the company's decision making as a whole is enhanced.

Carry on regardless

Modern management gurus make much of the need for innovation. New products and services keep a company young and enthusiastic. In principle we must agree with them. The problem is that change can become attractive for its own sake. This is dangerous. Someone has got to keep on making the core product more profitably until the new one pays off. Even if you have not got a cash cow, you need to keep a large slice of the team in blinkers doing what they know how, even better than last year, if today's profits are to be earned. By all means let a small team innovate, but if everyone starts looking to the future who is minding the shop?

A good example was a doomed product in a declining market. There was going to be no innovation for growth, just inventive ways of slowing the decline. All the group's planning for growth was taking place in other companies concerned with other products. The local team settled down and started to take advantage of the known facts in a way that their competitors did not. They increased their market penetration and their profitability several years in a row, as the market declined inexorably. They ended up as market leader, with a very firm grip on the residual and continuing UK market. It is not a coincidence that the company was part of Hanson Trust.

Negative planning

Previous sections have looked at various attitudes to planning; lots of companies don't have financial planning or indeed any form of forward planning. Some avoid it because they are afraid of it. Others don't believe it possible to plan effectively in volatile markets and economic conditions. There can be some sympathy for them; where the forward planning exercise is essentially speculative and subject to frequent change, as new views of future possibilities flit by, there is often more confusion than enlightenment.

There is an alternative. Even if you cannot decide what is going to happen, you may be able to plan what to avoid. This exercise can also be very useful in acquisition studies. The amount of time wasted researching possible acquisitions which turn out to be unacceptable to a board for reasons long known and never codified must be massive.

There are other parameters. Even in a company where you cannot forecast revenue, you ought to be able to monitor overheads and establish a target for revenue which will tell you whether you are above or below breakeven point. This is infinitely preferable to the head in the sand attitude which tempts people to wait until the year has finished, unplanned and unsung, before finding out whether they did it right.

One analogy which comes readily to hand is the currency snake. The snake in the tunnel sounds alarms when it touches the tunnel walls. This is precisely what the negative planning concept does in profit matters – to blow a whistle when the unacceptable area is reached in revenue or expense terms.

Negative planning is not exception reporting. The latter is based on fuller budgets and plans, but only deviations are highlighted. With negative planning you only highlight gross deviations, but you do so without the detailed earlier plans.

Even if you cannot decide what is going to happen, you may be able to plan what to avoid.

Inaction

The alternative least often considered in forward planning is doing nothing. Once a mood of change has gripped management, it is very difficult to be the one to say 'Whoa there' and start debating how the status quo might be tuned rather than spending all that money.

The same applies to revenue, expense and capital investment analysis. One of the most useful people in management is the manager who is prepared to take a little flak now and then for asking the negative and reactionary questions. That manager may end up being called a dog in the manger, but some of the time the attitude will be right. I have even seen boards of directors busily addressing themselves to a major acquisition necessitated by forecast future market expansion when the previous item on the agenda was a current downturn in sales in the very product for which they were about to increase capacity. Fortunately the board included a devil's advocate prepared to argue for inaction.

A retired policeman and a dog

If a company has developed the right approach for making money, it should not then throw it all away. Most companies are insecure, in one way or another. Crime has magnified, in volume and 'quality' in recent years. So have the defences available.

What has not changed enough is the acceptance of 'security management' as a key function in public companies. Too often, security is regarded as a small piece of the company secretary's role or a low-level function at the gate, equipped with a retired policemand and an anti-social dog.

A brief review of the range and scope of possible losses should serve to dispel the idea that it can in any way be a secondary function. Security in its widest sense covers all the things listed, and it includes many things which could cause or precipitate the total closure of the organisation. Only the managing director's brief is more onerous in this respect.

The assessment of risk and the decision whether to aim for total prevention, neglect plus insurance, self-insurance, partial avoidance and/or controlled panic (after the event) for each category of risk are extremely sensitive areas of management. A business which does not do the analysis may be very cheerful and may even run more profitably when times are good, but the downside risk is so huge that risk assessment is virtually essential, even if you eventually decide to compromise about the risks identified. At least, when ruin stares you in the face, you will be able to yield gracefully.

A low-level function at the gate . . .

The differing roles of security and insurance need to be considered and security should come first. Few managing directors like creating additions to their headcount budgets, but the expenditure of a five figure sum on a security manager may well be preferable to collecting the insurance monies (and suffering the resulting four or five figure increase in premium). Most companies have insurance well under control. Risks are insured or a deliberate decision has been made to 'self-insure'. In most big groups there is probably a full-time insurance manager, but not a security manager at a senior level. Logically, this is a rotten assessment of priorities. Security management is the primary line of defence. Insurance is a backstop when security fails. Often they are treated in reverse order, with security action as a sop to the insurers and no primary effort being taken to prevent insured risks (or the uninsured) turning into massive claims (or uninsured losses). Surely you would rather avoid having your foot mangled than collect a lump sum on your PA policy? Does not the same principle apply to the pillars of your corporate establishment?

Direct Losses

Removal of: Cash
                 Products
                 Fixed assets
                 Consumable stores
                 Employees' property
                 Confidential or complex original data

Damage to: The above, plus corporate records, by bomb, arson, vandalism, sabotage or accident

Fraud: Of all kinds

Other Losses

Industrial espionage
Kidnapping
Accidental disclosure of confidential data
Assaults upon employees, customers or visitors
Radiation
Poisoning
Asphyxiation
Fire injuries
Flood (drowning and contamination)
Loss of business by industrial action—including boycott, picketing and so on

---

The perfect crime

Bad management is the breeding ground for the perfect crime, and many big companies have given birth to it. The criteria these perfectionists have to meet are as follows:

1. Nobody feels victimised, which usually demands a large corporate victim.
2. There is no evidence, or the evidence is capable of an innocent interpretation.
3. The 'crime' is not discovered (and if discovered, will not be disclosed to the police).
4. There are no accomplices who might confess to misbehave.
5. The sums involved are massive enough to justify the effort and risk.

The cases which have filtered to the public or specialised press in recent years demonstrate that one person and a computer can achieve much of this in many environments. Earlier in this book it was demonstrated that someone can easily commit crime without a computer. All that is needed is a place in the accounts to hide the loss! One of two things must be true. Either you bury your 'drawings' in a much bigger loss which nobody analyses thoroughly or something worthless must be accepted as a substitute for something valuable. Once the numbers get big enough, people don't analyse properly. The 'bad management' behaviour here is the acceptance of the unanalysable.

Once upon a time, as a senior financial analyst doing the monthly profit performance report for Ford of Britain's car sales, I employed the most sophisticated analysis on every conceivable item in the sales records, with the exception of one figure – the KD Omits. These were the items left out of the packs of knocked down vehicles being exported, because the president of Ruritania owned a tyre factory, or a premier's second cousin made batteries, or it was genuinely more economic to make uphostery locally.

I was worried about the KD Omits. Past experience in the Tractor Division led me to wonder whether any genius, with or without a computer facility, was stuffing imaginary entries into the unanalysed balancing figure which made up this loss of revenue. On closer examination I stopped worrying. There was no net unaccounted loss in KD Omits, because the balancing figure turned out to be a profit, every month, every year. Nobody in the United States queried it. I still do not know where the extra money was coming from. Perhaps, if it's still going on, someone will check and let me know. The message remains. If it's big enough, credible enough and unanalysable, someone will drive a tunnel into it and start mining for gold.

To take another motor example – you would imagine that Ford could count and account for built-up motor cars. Back in the 1960s in the audit function, we did. Vehicles leaving the premises were subject to the most stringent checks and paperwork as they went from us to delivery agent to dealer. The only nagging doubt in my mind was that I wanted a Lotus Cortina and there were allegedly none to be had, yet there had been two virginal examples sitting in the delivery agents' compound, in deep wax, for weeks on end. We checked. The manufacturing paperwork existed but nobody had bothered to check why no delivery documentation had been processed to trigger off the invoice routine. We checked further. In all, over four hundred beautiful shining new Ford cars had been built but not invoiced. Some were lingering in compounds, some had reached dealers but not been invoiced and some hundred odd had vanished for ever, perhaps to one hundred opportunists, perhaps to a young man with a program.

There is no happy ending. We never found them. I never got my Lotus Cortina. And the nice man in the Employee Vehicle Sales Department who was teeming and lading furiously got caught by accident while all the fuss was going on!

Bad management is an excellent smokescreen for good crime. But nothing is too big or too uncontrollable to be analysed. If it is, you are halfway to being out of business. The thefts may not get you, but the 'legal' losses will.

To take our final example, do you have in your corporate 'chart of accounts' a heading for 'sundries' or 'miscellaneous'? Most of us do. Should we? Its existence suggests several things – that we are too lazy to analyse, that our classifications are imprecise or that the purpose of the expenditure is unclear.

If we cannot classify it, why are we spending it? Once we are forced to classify expenditure properly, the perfect crime becomes more difficult.

4
Communication rules – OK?

With the right attitudes, the right people and the right approach to making money good communication is the final ingredient in good management. Looking for mistakes, most bad management includes elements of bad communication. But in problems of communication diagnosis will not guarantee a cure, for three reasons.

First, some managers are incapable of understanding and practising good communication, because they have spent all their lives perfecting the bad.

Second, some managers can understand good communication, but they decide there are good reasons for avoiding it, at all costs. Or they 'haven't time'.

Third, many managers are competent and eager to communicate well, but they work for managers who cannot or will not.

Just in case you think you and your company are communicating properly already, test yourself with the following questions:
1. When the board or managers reject a carefully reasoned proposal are the reasons for rejection:
   – equally carefully reasoned?
   – communicated explicitly to the group which produced the proposal?
2. Are your telephonist and receptionist the nicest, most helpful and most informative people in the whole of your support staff (and paid accordingly)?

3. Do all your support staff know enough about your product/service to retain and increase the interest of a possible buyer who visits unexpectedly or telephones in?
4. Do all your staff know why:
   – the company exists?
   – your job exists?
   – their job exists?
5. Does anyone review outgoing correspondence, from all levels, to identify negative attitudes and damaging practices? Very much 'Big Brother is Watching You' but how else do you find who is rowing backwards?
6. Have you surplus production capacity which improved sales performance could mop up? If so, is it perceived as a communication problem?
7. Are you conscious of even one senior manager whose contacts with the outside world are less than satisfactory. If so (and most companies have one) it is unlikely that anyone has bothered to quantify the damage being done. Worse, although there will have been mutterings, nobody has bothered to consider whether a remedy is possible or indeed if the culprit would be happier cured. It is rather like the original Lifebuoy ads. Best friends won't tell, because it is (almost) unmentionable. If the potential damage is serious, doing nothing is not an acceptable course of action. The one ray of light is that nobody may have to tell, because there are three possible cures, only one of which demands disclosure:
   – in-house training for *all* managers.
   – external training, as part of a larger programme.
   – if the culprits are reasonable and well-balanced, tell them tactfully, authoritatively and supportively. Train if required.

Finally, there is only one question to ask. Are you communicating with yourself? Most management problems are caused by people who fail to recognise and face the implications of the things they already know.

Gossip abhors a vacuum

We all know about nature and vacuums. Alas, managements seldom realise that the principle applies to all absences of information within a company. The Industrial Society has been preaching for many years the need for good communications within a company, to an extent which should have covered, or at the very least touched, every manager in the UK. It may have touched them but it has all too often passed on by.

Are you communicating with yourself?

The problem is that if employees do not have information about what is happening above and around them, they can invent it. In some cases this consists of using their initiative and guessing, or analysing, what is happening and why it is happening (useful if it keeps the place going, dangerous if they guess wrong). In other cases it involves going off into inspired flights of fancy, with wild and wholly baseless speculation about the attitudes and actions of people who, if they knew, would be horrified. It is sad that what they would be horrified about is the gossip, not the fact that they, in management, had left a gap for gossip to flow into.

In one recent case a company thought it had done a reasonable job communicating with its management team (10% of the total employee strength) who were invited to regular meetings to hear about company plans, reasons why past decisions had been taken, progress on major capital projects, sneak previews on profits and a mass of other hot news. To the board's surprise, a communications audit disclosed that the rest of the staff felt that they were kept in the dark. Too many well-kept secrets were around, according to the mass. There was a missing link. Nobody had bothered to tell the fortunate 10% which aspects of the disclosure they could or should disseminate. They *all* assumed all the communications were privileged and should be kept from their subordinates. The rest of the communications audit results showed the quality of misinformation which had flowed in to fill the gap.

Effective writing

Anyone who has been faced by a mass of curriculum vitaes generated by a vacancy, even at a senior level, will have wondered why people do not apply to their career histories the same standard of preparation they apply to the preparation of professional reports. But, taking a closer look, we probably do give the same standards to c.v.'s that we allocate to other documents. That is why both are frequently lousy. The same ground rules must apply to all documentation.

The first rule must be to consider whether any form of communication is required at all. If it is, one should consider whether it should be written or verbal (it could also be pictorial, filmed, videotaped, gestured, symbolic or physical, but I think we must exclude the more extreme examples).

The next essential is to define the purpose of the document. The purpose of any solicited or unsolicited communication has a considerable effect on its content and presentation, but few think fully about the context in which they are writing. There are at least five reasons for originating business paperwork; to inform, to generate action, to entertain, to create a necessary formal record and to comply with a statute without doing any of the other four. The information category is the largest, including:

1. Teaching.
2. Conveying information leading to and requiring a decision. (This can be neutral or designed to achieve a particular decision. If the latter the whole document falls in a different category.)

3. Conveying data, requiring no decisions.
4. Rebutting, discussing or answering prior documents. (This category needs to be distinguished from 2 and 3, though there is some overlap.)
5. Clearing one's own mind by committing matters to paper. (One has to be careful this does not fall into another category by inadvertent disclosure. If so, the rules apply fully.)

If you fail to define the reasons correctly, you may generate the wrong response to the document. A c.v., for instance, is seldom just meant to convey data. It is often a marketing document, i.e., it conveys information requiring a decision. A document leading to a decision which fails to generate one is not a success. Its structure can often be the reason. A document meant merely to convey data, which instead generates a gratuitous and possibly unwelcome decision has similarly failed.

In fact any document which is wrongly categorised by its originator and therefore wrongly presented is likely to produce an incorrect response. For instance, answers to questions which are indistinguishable from a voluntary statement permit the reader to take them out of context. It is seldom the fault of the reader. Murphy's law applies – if the thing is capable of misinterpretation, someone somewhere is sure to misinterpret it.

Having decided what one is producing, the next essential must be to devise a format which ensures that the thing gets read (or not, depending on one's intentions) by even the most obtuse reader one wishes to affect. There is a crude maxim for speeches 'Tell them what you're going to tell them. Tell them. Tell them you've told them'. Converted into formal documentation this normally demands an introduction (and contents list or index), a main body of text and a conclusion. (Appendices are often necessary but in principle undesirable. If there is anything important in them the key bits should form part of the text whenever feasible.)

The conclusion is often the only piece that some readers will absorb (or even read). To foster this, if appropriate, the conclusion can be reproduced in isolation at the front of the package. If it is desirable that people read and absorb the body of the text, an informative index and informative section headings work wonders. Compare the two examples. 'A' is guaranteed to reduce the effective readership. 'B' seems likely to guarantee 100% attention. Yet they describe the same report.

Example A

————The Future of the Slagflump Industry————

1. Scope of the Study, and Constraints
2. Economic Factors
3. Political Factors
4. Competition
5. Supply, labour and Related Matters
6. Likely Courses for the Industry
7. Conclusion and Recommendations

Example B

The Uncertain Future of the Slagflump Industry and this Group

1. Scope of this study, and constraints
2. Adverse economic trends
3. Probable serious political problems
4. Unacceptable levels of competition in key markets
5. Inevitable raw materials, fuel and labour shortages forecast
6. Probable contraction of the industry and suggested diversification
7. Recommendations for the immediate reorganisation of the group's major activities

The rules for creating good text could fill a book (and do: *Complete Plain Words*, Sir Ernest Gowers, published by Penguin, is recommended), but one can summarise. The scope of the paper needs to be specified. You understand it, others may not. The paper needs to be written in clear unequivocal English whose tone in each section conveys not just the fact but the atmosphere. For instance, if you are endeavouring to get a constructive and favourable response from the reader it is far better to say 'The majority of the proposals are fully acceptable, subject to discussion on the terms of paragraphs 3, 7 and 8', than 'the terms of the key paragraphs 3, 7 and 8 make the proposals impossible to accept'.

If you want to generate optimism, use warm adjectives and adverbs, use creative, positive verbs. For instance, not 'We could find no errors in the accounts', which is grudging and ungracious, but 'the accuracy of the accounting appears high'.

Factual accuracy is obviously necessary; when you are generalising, say so. Quote sources and the limitations of a sample where appropriate. Brevity in everything helps. There is no merit in length. If a fifty page report could be presented on one sheet of A4, it should be. The same applies to one's c.v. The one page career history has more impact than the brochure. Quite a few candidates submit bound brochures as their c.v.'s. Counterproductive, of course.

If you want action, or a decision, request it expressly or by implication in the text. The document is your sales representative, and every representative aims to close a sale. If you do not ask, you cannot expect to get.

Although it is important to be positive, if the document is to have a major impact anywhere, it should be seen to be fair. Consider all alternatives, however unacceptable, even if you dismiss them in the act of mentioning them. This is particularly true if you are presenting the results of impartial research on which you genuinely do not want to prejudge the issue. If someone can assume one omission in your research, the whole document is discredited. In this context, most people forget that doing nothing is *always* an alternative and sometimes, rightly or wrongly, a very attractive one. It panders to the 'Why don't we just wait and see . . .' attitude of apathetic, incompetent, indecisive or frightened management.

Most management is incompetent in some respect and every kind of incompetence is likely to be reflected in attitudes to documentary presentations. The optimum reader is rare. You are writing for the less than perfect. You have to compensate for their possible deficiencies. I am sure you have been present when two sane intelligent people are conversing and think they are communicating, when both are achieving the worst possible distortions of each others remarks. You want to bang their heads together and make them start again. Similar failures are daily evident in the correspondence columns of *The Times*, in solicitors' client files, Inland Revenue correspondence and a multiplicity of other documents.

There is a way round this problem, which demands personal discipline or a helpful friend. If you can get someone impartial to proof read, do so. If not, try actively to *misread* things yourself. Finally, ask again whether the contents of every document could be better presented in another form – perhaps verbally, perhaps graphically. What seemed right when you were writing the detail of it can be horribly wrong as a composite whole. For this reason it is unwise to write anything when one is incensed and there is seldom any merit in reacting emotionally in writing to a prior document which has itself been badly or emotionally written.

Brevity is the whole of it

One of the greatest obstacles to good managerial communication is that most managers have some inkling of the need to communicate. This is possibly the best working example of the old saying 'a little knowledge is a dangerous thing', because bad managers leap readily from the desert of non-communication to the morass of over-communication.

The basic lesson to learn and try to apply is that communication failures increase in direct proportion to the volume of material communicated. Most of us recognise this in principle, but cannot make the connection between the principle and our personal worlds. In consequence, we overflow from one necessary page to a second counterproductive one. We fail to attempt any precis. We write for effect, rather than objective. We produce stylised reports which invite filing or destruction rather than action.

You know the principles, but if we restate them we are better equipped to reexamine them:

1. Words are generally more compelling than raw numbers.
2. One cogent phrase is better than several paragraphs.
3. One picture is allegedly worth a thousand words.

So it goes on. We need relatively few pages – ideally one; relatively few ideas per page – preferably grouped into a few main categories; relatively few words in each section – preferably simple words.

You could reasonably argue that you don't know how many words fit on one typescript A4 page. Anyone who hasn't got some idea of this figure is managing blindfold. It should be one of the first things you learn if you want to write effectively. The moment your victims (or addressees, in polite society) have to turn a page, you risk losing their interest. It is no use arguing that you have to write ten pages to explain the matter to them (or do you mean, to yourself?) if you lose them after the second sheet. It is absolutely vital that you give enough information on one page to permit them to understand your message, to seduce them into reading the rest or to let them appreciate the consequences of ignoring it. Even when you have done this, the obligation to achieve brevity in the rest remains with you.

Think how easy it is to remember the brief epigrams of Churchill, Coward, Wilde. Will your message survive equally well?

Four letter words

Short words are clear, long ones less so. Many of those whom you want to reach with words do not read *The Times*. They read *The Sun*. Too many long words and they will not read your notice/memo/ad.

The counter-argument, which bad managers employ to themselves or critics, is that it is uniquely difficult to express essential business concepts in simpler language and specifically in an appreciably truncated vocabulary.

I'm sorry, I'll say that again: 'It is very hard to say things about work more simply and to use short basic words'.

You will note that the first and third paragraphs consist almost entirely of monosyllabic words of four letters or less. The second paragraph, to the literate manager, should be more precise in its meaning and richer in its use of the English language. Both are luxuries we cannot afford if they lose us readers or comprehension.

Any document which is intended to reach a representative cross-section of the population demands a massive effort by its author to use very basic English. There is no option, if you are writing to be understood rather than for the pleasure of reading your own words. It is an effort, but it becomes easier after some practice.

There is a bonus. If you are forced to use very simple language, you are also forced to use fairly simple concepts, with less opportunity for studied imprecisions, euphemisms and the other deceits of 'educated' writing. The enforced clarity might even improve communications in other media or on other occasions.

Annual reports

Most corporate annual reports are:
– Boring
– Costly
– Incomprehensible
– Insulting and
– Wrongly aimed.
For evidence, look at your own company's latest example.

There is a very good reason why most are bad. They are required by statute. They become an obligation rather than an opportunity. (In the same way that Government documents, because they are a statutory obligation, are prepared with no regard for reader or user.) The creator forgets the possible audience and instead adds cosmetic touches to the statutory core, whereas the law is remarkably flexible, and it would be equally possible to design the ideal annual report and check that it includes the statutory bits, rather than the other way.

69

An annual report is going to be read by a very wide audience, who can be influenced in a way achieved by no other document, not least because its obligatory nature and certification by the auditor enhances its authority. It offers a chance to reach not only the shareholders, but also bankers, customers, employees and potential employees, future investors, suppliers, union officials and the stock exchanges.

Every time management puts together an annual report without adequate attention to this audience an opportunity to do something constructive is missed and, by neglect, something damaging may creep in instead.

You should find opportunities for at least one of the following improvements.

Language
Is the text intelligible to your least intelligent literate employee? If not, some of the shareholders will not understand it. Some stockbrokers may have trouble too. It takes a conscious effort to use short clear words and avoid jargon, but it must be worth it.

Attitudes
Does the report fulminate against the unions or government? Far too many do and thus perpetuate a 'them and us' attitude in industrial relations. If the chairman has a grudge against the unions constructive action should be taken to improve relations and the unions' understanding of the business, not to alienate them by moaning in print to an embarrassingly large audience. Every chairman who makes such comments in print is also recording a degree of management failure. Somebody ought to be suggesting an alternative which carries a more constructive message.

Sales
Several groups of people who read the report may be sympathetic to the company and tempted to buy its products and services, provided thay are clearly identified. Does the report also tell them where and how to get them? (Branch telephone numbers? National chain stockists?) I recall one superb new service which I was tempted to use and which, according to the company, was in every Yellow Pages nationwide. Sadly, they omitted to record what classification it was hiding under. I still haven't found it.

Statutory rubbish
This is not exempt from the suggestions above. It does not have to be in traditional layout, conservative vocabulary or accounting jargon. There is also no law about graphic aids, of all kinds. 'Pop-up' models and perhaps even a tape cassette might aid understanding of the printed word!

Newsletter
If you don't send a newsletter to employees, the annual report could to some extent be one. If you do issue one regularly, the annual report could be part of it. This has the additional merit that it may be cheaper to print and more people (including more shareholders) may read it. Why shouldn't it look like *The Sun* or, if you feel conservative, *The Mail* or *Express*?

Help
The fund of goodwill among readers may be wider than as potential customers. If in the next twelve months you know you want to procure new premises, services, raw materials, people, companies or even products, why not say so? There will be occasions when it is commercially inadvisable, but there will be many more when people out there will welcome the chance to help/supply/quote/join. And it is free advertising.

Finally, if you run a private company and congratulate yourself that you don't have this problem, your real problem is that you are ignoring an opportunity.

MIS

The initials above usually mean management information systems. This is a misnomer. Certainly they describe systems. Certainly these contain information. Unfortunately many of these do not inform management.

MIS should mean Minimum Information Systems and be used as such. There is then some possibility that they would be fit for use by management.

Why shouldn't it look like 'The Sun'?

A rule of management science is required: 'Comprehension varies inversely from the volume of data involved'. Those who have worked in companies where the monthly performance reports are half an inch thick can probably appreciate that the level of understanding at board level is slim. The addition of a very simple management summary, with simple pictures and charts showing only key variances, dramatically improved the quality and nature of queries and action flowing after board meetings. There may even be a 'problem of the month' spot, which demands management attention to something which conventional channels are not solving. It works. One set of specialist directors, who had previously said that an engineering change could not be achieved in under nine months, got it through in under six weeks when the attention of the rest of the board was concentrated properly upon the real problem.

Excess information does not inform. It obscures. So does reporting of situations normal. Exception reporting informs better than total reporting. Try it and get better results with minimum effort.

Junk mail

Most of us receive junk mail. It is easy to recognise. With practice you can detect it quickly and transfer it at once to your waste paper basket. This is not the problem. My concern is that you and other managers may be *writing* junk mail on a large scale. The commercial people who send volume mailings are happy with a minority response. You cannot afford it when you are sending one-off letters. A 90% failure rate is unacceptable. Even 10% must be. You need a 100% success rate and it is very unlikely that you are getting it. Few people write effective business letters, memos, notices and internal correspondence.

To demonstrate this, let us take the junk mail example further. Among the unsolicited items in my incoming mail there is always a minority of book club offers, cooking card schemes, overpriced mail order tat catalogues, personalised credit card invitations and exciting news about free gifts I have allegedly already won (I always apply – they never arrive). Some can be identified on sight and dumped unopened. Others can be opened just to check for paperclips – the only true free gift.

I therefore make three qualitative checks. The first is to see whether the sender has given enough information for me to reject the envelope out of hand. The second is a preliminary scan of the contents to find signs which justify rejection without really reading any of it. Only if these tests fail do I look for a compelling reason to read the thing more fully.

Analyse your own reactions to the next examples you get and you may find your system is similar. Worse, the people you write to may use similar principles and extend them to their review of your business missives. Even if you are at the top of your corporate heap and it's a big heap, your name only commands respect when they know it's you. Boredom can set in before they reach your name.

Traditional business communications are usually defective in some way. If you want to get a message across in writing you have to do much more than assemble all the thoughts and words at random on the page, as they fall out of your head. Nor is it enough to follow the dictates of 'business layout'. There is something to learn from the Time-Lifes and Readers Digests of this world. You may not like their letters, but they do have impact. They have several objectives, all of which are valid for your individual business correspondence, if you want it to be opened promptly and read, rather than scrapped or filed.

These objectives are:

1. Identify addressees.
2. Address them by name.
3. Tempt them to open the envelope soon.
4. Seduce them into reading the text fully.
5. Provoke or sway them to action or response.
6. Make it clear what action or response is wanted.
7. Make it easy to act.

All the above may seem commonsense – but do you attempt it, let alone achieve it, in practice? For a start, do you always consider whether you are writing to the right person? The natural temptation is to write to the easiest target, the most high ranking, the one you know best or the one you want to hurt, impress or confuse. If instead you go a step further and ask what results you want to achieve, the addressee you have to choose will often not be the one you first thought of. The principle of writing for results applies whether you are dealing with customers, suppliers, advisers, bankers or ten thousand potential buyers.

Addressing them by name may also be obvious, but how often do we fail to? It is so easy to omit the name on letter or envelope, to make do with title alone, to generate an impersonal salutation in consequence and by doing so ensure that the letter is not read willingly, or in some cases, at all. Titles are not only impersonal, they become obsolete. If you actually need to reach a particular individual rather than a particular job-holder, using the last known title may confuse rather than help. If you want to reach someone holding down a specific job, check who the current job-holder is, so that you can compel attention with his or her name. Finally, remember that envelopes get parted from letters in mailrooms. Get the detail right on both.

Now what else can we do to tempt the recipient to open the envelope on receipt? How can we get the contents to him intact? First class stamps help. The words Personal, Private and Confidential also help, provided the contents are not so tedious as to provoke deeper contempt at the misuse of a P&C description.

So far, so good. They are looking at the first page (which is ideally the last, as well . . .). They know it is addressed to them. Can we hold their attention? Do we really try? This drags us back to the point about results. A spurious bid for attention, unrelated to the reason for writing, may fail. You must command attention and lead it towards those results. All documents need to be structured in this way, but the effort is wasted if you do not compel continuing attention. One way to do so is to title your first page, yet how many letters you write and receive have headings or side headings? How many tell you in the first sentence why they have been written and therefore why anyone should bother to read them?

If you can produce a compelling heading and a powerful first sentence, they may bother. If you cannot have both, for heaven's sake have one or other.

The next practical bit is trying to use just one page of A4, testing every sentence to see whether it is brief, necessary, relevant and constructive . . . and in the right place. If in the course of this exercise you cannot spot one which is overlong, redundant, tautologous or misplaced I shall be surprised.

Where were we? Where were you? We would know if we had charted our way beforehand. I recommend a large sheet of scrap paper. Scribble the ideas in a circle. Then link them with a logical line, ruthlessly delete the unnecessary and highlight the essentials. Lead to a final action paragraph which so many letters lack:

1. Ask for a decision.
2. Ask for a firm order.
3. Request a response, information, or a remittance.
4. Give a specific instruction.
5. Tempt, provoke, seduce or direct response.

If you can achieve none of these, why are you bothering to write at all?

Finally, look at the finished product and imagine your response if you were receiving it, at arm's length, from someone with no claim on your goodwill – whether within your organisation or outside – would you be gratuitously offended, pleased, informed, provoked to respond or just apathetic? If you can't be that impartial, ask your secretary. Secretaries have opinions which they often keep to themselves. Their second opinion can be your saving grace.

Bad form

One easy way to test for bad management in any organisation is to look at any form it publishes for outsiders to complete. Internal forms are almost equally good as an indicator, but there is more excuse for their inadequacies, and they are not evidence of the organisation's attitude to the world. Good external forms are good PR.

How do you assess whether a form is 'bad' in this context? There is no great art to it. As a layman you are well equipped to test, provided you are not an in-company user of the completed form and therefore inured to its defects.

A simple checklist might run as follows:
1. Are the typefaces easily legible?
2. Is the form reasonably brief?
3. Does it explain itself clearly, in simple words?
4. Are all of the questions incapable of misinterpretation as sexist or racist?
5. Does it encourage and aid completion?
6. Does it explain why peripheral information is asked for?
7. Does its phraseology avoid gratuitous offence to the form-filler?
8. Are the 'Office Use Only' bits clearly separate from the rest and devoid of offensive matter?
9. If it has to be returned by post, does it show the return address clearly? (Could it usefully be post free?)
10. Has it apparently been reviewed against the possibility that changes in the law have made it obsolete or illegal?

If you can generate ten affirmative replies, you are looking at a pretty good form. If not, the organisation issuing it is suffering from one of two problems:

1. Nobody realises or cares about the importance of forms design in corporate PR.
2. They realise, but they are too arrogant or reactionary to identify the errors.

Just in case you are reviewing your own forms and you are broad-minded enough to realise that you could be blind to their defects, there is a further test. Find out whether significant numbers are never completed, partially completed, wrongly completed, returned late or accompanied by rude comments.

Every bit of paper which the organisation issues has at least two objectives. The primary ones are very varied. The secondary one is always part of your corporate public relations effort. Good forms are 'house advertising'. They can even help sell specific products and services to a captive audience. It isn't just bad management to ignore this. It is sabotage.

Is the form reasonably brief?

Phone blocks

If you are incompetent in your handling of telephone conversations, you might as well be illiterate or lacking in numeracy. For a modern manager the fault is heinous and unprofessional. Every telephone call can have a certain beauty of structure which works for you. It is theoretically simple. The parties connect, identify themselves and the subject matter, discuss it, resolve it toward a decision or request for further information, and then close. The failures arise because people do not keep to the rules.

The opening gambit is simple. You dial the number of your victim and wait for the phone to be answered. If you are answering the phone, always give your name, or company name, or number when you receive a call. Anything less is an insult to the caller. It is now the caller's turn to state their name, fuller identification, ask for their victim and if appropriate state their business.

At this point the competent callers start to gain their advantage over the incompetent. They will have started the call determined to be nice to operators, secretaries, PA's, and wrong numbers in the victim's building – on the principle that they may be stupid, new, temporary or just plain bad-tempered, but nevertheless they are the only channel to the victim. They will also remember they have no right to access. They are trespassers or visitors on licence. However, they can do a lot to improve the situation. For instance, they can say 'John Smith please. My name is Jones, Eric Jones' if they are on first name terms and have reached a secretary or a *small* PBX. They can point out that they are returning a call, or replying to a letter. Both will improve their chances. It is also courteous to give some idea of the matter for discussion unless it is incredibly confidential. Someone who will not state their business risks being taken for a life insurance salesman, blackmailer, headhunter or discourteous boor. (The four are not synonymous.) Another courtesy is to forecast the time one needs. Someone who says 'I need two minutes only, and it's fairly urgent' stands a good chance of getting through the barriers. If they keep to the time limit they also improve their chances for next time.

All this sounds like common sense. It is, but very few people fully observe the rules in practice. They lose half their wits the moment they pick up a telephone, and their latent defects all emerge at once. Forgive me also if I harp on the barriers. They can be considerable. Other things being equal, someone who has taken the trouble to visit in person has a moral claim to priority over the telephone caller. They do not always get it, but if you are on the phone you must expect some failures from this cause or from 'meetings', lunches and other absences. The telephone caller must recognise that the chances of making contact first time vary from 100% (on a direct line) to 10%. For example, in my business we have callers who have not even bothered to think how our business runs. A typical week must include nearly twenty hours of client or candidate meetings plus preparation of advertisements, job descriptions and candidate reports to a very tight time schedule. This inevitably means that the casual visitor or phone caller stands less than a one in five chance of reaching us at any time.

The next phase, when you fail to make contact, is to leave a valid message. This applies whether or not you want action from the victim. From their point of view there are few things more perplexing than to hear that twelve people phoned, would not leave a message and would not give their names. (This could be twelve people with trivial matters to discuss, six people worried enough to phone twice, four worried people phoning thrice or two desperate people phoning every half hour for three hours!)

The message may be just to say 'Fred phoned, said it wasn't urgent and will phone later' or it may be a full and informative text. If it is intended to be the latter, can we please have some intelligent thought exercised? For a start, a request to return a call is *not* a complete message. Unless the subject matter and urgency are blindingly obvious from the context, they should be explicitly stated. Anything less is an imposition on the victim and leads to the establishment of incorrect priorities. In my system, client companies take precedence, so candidates' messages need to be carefully structured to achieve action. They have to contain a certain core of data and yet be capable of accurate transcription by the standard low IQ message bearer at the victim's end. This means keeping it simple, avoiding difficult words, spelling nouns, reading back *all* numbers and shunning long sentences. As an example, one of my typical incoming messages might read 'Mr Rees *is* interested in the job you wrote about and *does* wish to be considered for the shortlist'. At first sight this looks sensible. In fact, it is unsatisfactory. There are a lot of Reeses in the world (and Reiths) so initials would be helpful. A reference number or the name of the job or company would help and the date of my letter would also assist. As it is Mr Rees/Reith/Reeve? may have caused us a lot of unnecessary work.

When the initial call or the messages have finally borne fruit and the principals are finally ear to ear, the worst disasters are perpetrated. Have you ever noticed how, the moment you hear the person you want, all the points for discussion vanish from your mind and you review one point only and then chat about the weather for five minutes. If this is your problem, have a checklist to hand before you dial. The same applies if you expect a complex incoming call. I also keep a massive diary in which I record every significant incoming and outgoing call – or projected call, so I can assess priorities and nag myself to complete the day's calls in good time. It helps, even for a disorganised lazy incompetent like me. Incidentally – one final thought on this subject – you now understand the deeper reasons for the classic theatre line: 'Don't call us, we'll call you'.

The last word

Finally, the most constructive message. This book has been about learning from (and avoiding) mistakes. Although this is not a negative concept, it has forced us to view rather too many negative examples.

Where communication is concerned, this is not enough. For the successful manager, we revert to the words of the song 'Accentuate the Positive'. As a successful manager-communicator *you* have to reach out across the barriers of apathy and incomprehension, bridge the gaps, plug the loopholes, cross the t's and dot the i's, to ensure that *your* messages get through, *your* objectives are attained and, incidentally, *your* career flourishes! Be better than the uncaring and unobservant and it surely will.